GREEN SLAM

Ireland's Grand Slam 2009

Born in Strabane, Co Tyrone, Stephen McGarrigle is a graduate of Liverpool Business School. He lives in London, where he works as a civil servant. He lives with his partner and has three sons. This is his fourth book. Previous publications include *Manchester United – The Irish Connection; Green Gunners – Arsenal's Irish and A Complete Who's Who of Irish International Football*. He has worked in television, as a pundit on *Talksport* and helped research and narrate a BBC documentary on the 1958 Munich Air Crash.

GREEN SLAM

Ireland's Grand Slam 2009

Stephen McGarrigle

GREEN SLAM

Ireland's Grand Slam 2009

Olympia Publishers
London

www.olympiapublishers.com
OLYMPIA PAPERBACK EDITION

A CIP catalogue record for this title is
available from the British Library.

ISBN: 978-1-84897-076-2

First Published in 2010

Olympia Publishers
60 Cannon Street
London
EC4N 6NP

Printed in Great Britain

CONTENTS

Acknowledgments

Thank you to all who have contributed to this volume and sincere apologies to anyone whose work is included but not acknowledged. This will have been a genuine oversight and I thank you retrospectively.

Special thanks to RBS6nations; scrum.com and lionsrugby.com who have kindly granted permission to plunder their archives which provided the foundation stone of this publication.

Thanks also to myriad rugby correspondents who have granted permission to use their expert scribblings for my research and education on oval ball matters. They are Duncan Bech (*Scotland on Sunday, The Guardian, The Herald, The Independent, The Scotsman, The Sunday Times*); David Walsh (*The Sunday* Times); Robert Kitson (*The Guardian, The Observer*); Brendan Fanning (*The Sunday Independent, Scotland on Sunday, The Guardian, The Observer*); Peter O'Reilly, (*The Times, The Sunday Times*); Roy Curtis; David Kelly (*The Independent, Irish Independent*); Stephen Jones, (*The Guardian, The Independent, The Sunday Times, The Times*); Rob Hodgetts (*BBC News*); John O'Sullivan (*The Daily Telegraph, The Sunday Telegraph, The Irish Times*); Peter Jackson (*MailOnline, The Scotsman, The Sunday Times*); John Westerby (*The Sunday Times, The Times*); Lyle Jackson (*BBC News*); Maire Ofeire (*The Bleacher Report);* Cormac O'Keefe (*Betfair*) and Edmund Van Esbeck for his memories of the 1948 campaign.

Last but not least thanks to Mr Ian Bendelow and Feargal Coffey at Smart Languages Solutions and to Paula M Doherty for the many hours spent poring over the manuscript.

Introduction

'I want to be under pressure, I want to be the favourite because I think that's what we are. I think we can be the best.'

Ireland Captain, Brian O'Driscoll

Mickey Mouse is probably the only mammal older than the monkey that has clung doggedly to the back of the Irish rugby team for nigh on 61 years. Finally, finally the obdurate furry beastie has been prised kicking and screaming, battered, bloodied and bruised from the back of the Irish national team and kicked firmly into touch by the right boot of the one and only Ronan O'Gara.

1948 was the year in which Ireland was declared a Republic, although contrary to popular opinion, the name of the country remained as Ireland or Eire and does so to this day. On February 18th that year Eamon de Valera, head of government since 1932, lost power to an opposition coalition and John A. Costello was appointed Taoiseach of Eire by President O'Kelly.

London hosted the Olympic Games; rationing was still in place; the Allies launched the Berlin airlift and London's Heathrow airport was opened. Oh, and Ireland won the only Grand Slam of their long history, which, given the quality of players that have graced the green shirt over the years, is almost mind-boggling.

Ireland's wait for a second Grand Slam and their first of the modern era was excruciatingly painful. It had been as fruitless as waiting for Padraig Harrington's first major. And then look what happened.

In the interim Ireland fans existed on comparatively paltry pickings. In February 1982 they beat Scotland 21-12 to win the Triple Crown for the first time since 1949. The Championship was claimed in 1985 and since then, on many, many occasions commentators have ventured the thought that 'this could be the year', as happened in 2003, 2004, 2005, 2006 and 2007. All came and went without a Grand Slam or even a Championship, leaving only Triple Crowns and an ever burgeoning collection of 'what ifs?'

Hammered by England in a Grand Slam decider in 2003, the Triple Crown was captured in 2004 for the first time in 19 years. That campaign saw newly crowned World Champions England put to the sword in their own back yard in what would be the first of four successive defeats of the Old Enemy.

The second defeat of England in that sequence (19-13) in March 2005 saw Ireland move into the top four in the world rankings for the first time since November 2003, just behind the big three from the southern hemisphere, thus making Ireland the Number 1 side in the Northern Hemisphere. Heady times indeed. But still no Championship.

Hopes of an elusive Championship were still alive, albeit on life support, up until the final Test of 2005, when Ireland capitulated to Wales in Cardiff. Incredibly it was Ireland's first defeat in the Welsh capital since 1983.

Another Triple Crown and a runners' up spot to France made 2006 yet another nearly year. However, the autumn internationals of that year (in which Ireland's ritual disembowelling of South Africa was followed by a 21-6 defeat of Australia, in what was undoubtedly one of the greatest ever performances from an Irish rugby team) gave Ireland back-to-back home wins over southern-hemisphere opposition for the first time in 40 years, had the country purring. These victories, which were followed by a clinical demolition of the Pacific Islands by a 'weakened side', and had Ireland, rugby fans and just maybe Gaelic and soccer fans thinking the unthinkable.

In 2007 Ireland lost out on the Championship agonisingly on points difference to France. Ireland finished level with France and scored more tries, but lost out on the title due to an injury time French try against Scotland in their final game to finish with a points difference better by four. Oh for the bonus point system adopted everywhere else in rugby!

Alas those landmark victories proved to be yet more false dawns and the Grand Slam proved as elusive as ever.

A real dose of reality was injected into Irish hearts following the disastrous 2007 World Cup campaign. Ireland's pool of players was said to be stronger than at any time in history. With real depth at hooker, in the second row, at flanker, in the centre and possibly even on the wing – yet they continued to fail to deliver. And, having dropped to fourth place in the 2008 Championship the IRFU ran out of patience with head coach Eddie O' Sullivan.

The team entered the 2009 competition with the disastrous World Cup campaign and the country's worst ever Six Nations campaign of 2008 as recent memories. On the flip side the team was buoyed by the boost of a new coach – Declan Kidney had been appointed as Eddie O'Sullivan's successor the previous August – a brace of good performances down under, and the respective triumphs for Munster and Leinster in the Heineken Cup and Magners League. With the Irish economy facing its worst crisis in decades the country once again found itself enveloped in an air of rugby optimism. Could Declan Kidney work his magic with Ireland as he had done on so many occasions with Munster? The feeling was that if he could get the best out of a talented squad then Ireland had a great chance, especially since this was to be one of the years when France and England were visitors to Dublin.

What follows is the story of what happened next. The tale of Herculean men and memorable matches in an unforgettable six weeks from 7th February to 21st March 2009.

The difficulty with the men recalled in this volume is that each and every one are worthy of a book all to themselves – let's hope I've done them justice.

Herein it is a tribute to them all: The Class of 2009, Ireland's Grand Slam heroes: Enjoy!

But first a look back at their illustrious predecessors of 1948 and how the clean sweep, no Grand Slams in those days, was achieved.

Five Nations 1948

When the Ireland rugby team set out on the Championship trail in January 1948 it was more in hope than in expectation. The seeds of doubt were sown following an indifferent performance against Australia at Lansdowne Road the previous December, when they were comprehensively beaten 16-3 by the tourists. Given that only three points were awarded for a try in those days gives some idea as to the severity of the defeat. The Ireland team on that day was:

Dudley Higgins, William McKee, Kevin Quinn, Patrick Reid, Kevin O'Flanagan, Jack Kyle, Ernest Strathdee, Jimmy Corcoran, Karl Mullen, Albert McConnell, Richard Wilkinson, Jimmy Nelson, Bill McKay, Ernie Keeffe and Desmond McCourt.

The format for the 1948 Five Nations was somewhat different to its 2009 counterpart. No two games were played on the same day and the Championship was dragged out over three months from the beginning of January to the end of March. Incidentally, Ireland's sequence of matches in 1948 mirrored that of 2009.

Stunned by the level of the reverse against Australia, the Irish selectors made sweeping changes to the line-up for the opening game against France. There were no fewer than six changes from the team humbled by the Wallabies. Jim McCarthy, the flame-haired flanker from the Dolphin club, was the one new cap in the side, being named in the back row.

France 6 Ireland 13

Stade Colombes, January 1st, 1948

As would be the case 61 years later, France provided Ireland's first hurdle. Only, on this occasion, the game was staged in Paris, at the Stade Colombes. Remarkably the game was held in midweek and on New Year's Day.

In the corresponding fixture in Dublin in 1947 Ireland had lost 12-8, consequently there was little confidence that this could be overturned on French soil. But reversed it was as Ireland made little of their underdogs' tag by running out 13-6 winners.

The aforementioned McCarthy marked an excellent debut with a try, while centre Paddy Reid and left winger Barney Mullan also weighed in with tries. Mullan landed two conversions from three.

And so the victors made their way home sitting proudly on top of the Five Nations table, but would have to wait a full six weeks for their next challenge.

If there were any unexpected emergencies to be dealt with during their travels the call "Is there a doctor in the house?" would have been met with a veritable scrum. Ireland's team at the time included five players who were either medical students or qualified doctors – the entire front row of Jimmy Corcoran, Karl Mullen and Arthur Albert (A. A.) McConnell; one more in the back row in Bill McKay and in the front, from which so much brilliance flowed, the incomparable Jack Kyle, the star turn in that sepia tinged team.

IRELAND: Dudley Higgins, Bertie O'Hanlon, William McKee, Patrick Reid, Barney Mullan, Jack Kyle, Ernie Strathdee (Capt.), Jimmy Corcoran, Karl Mullen, Albert McConnell, Colm Callan, Ernie Keefe, Bill McKay, James McCarthy and Bob Ager.

England 10 Ireland 11
Twickenham, February 14th, 1948

By the time Ireland arrived in London on St. Valentine's Day 1948, Wales headed the table having taken a draw and a win from their games with England and Scotland respectively. This meant that only Ireland could win the Triple Crown. In those days there was no talk about a Grand Slam, indeed not one contemporary report of the match mentioned it. The Triple Crown was the Holy Grail.

Ireland made several changes to the team that had beaten France. Jack Mattson replaced Dudley Higgins at full-back; Hugh de Lacy came in for Ernie Strathdee at scrum half; John Christopher Daly replaced Jimmy Corcoran at prop; Jimmy Nelson took over from Ernie Keeffe in the second row and Des O'Brien replaced Bob Agar at number 8. And although Ernie Strathdee had led the victors of Paris, he rescinded his captaincy to Karl Mullen who brought his own special leadership qualities to bear as Ireland sought to take another step towards only their third Triple Crown, having secured it in 1894 and 1899.

The game had many echoes of the same fixture in 2009. And the portents were not good on either occasion. Ireland had been humiliated 22-0 by England in Dublin 1947; and in 2008 were beaten 33-10 at Twickenham despite having raced to an early ten point lead.

In 1948 Ireland went 11 points ahead with tries from Jack Kyle, Bill McKay, William McKee and a conversion from the boot of Barney Mullan. Two successful conversions of Dickie Guest tries reduced the margin to a mere one point. As in 2009, the men in green clung on to win the match.

The result left Ireland once again sitting pretty at the top of the table on four points, with nearest challengers Wales on three, Scotland two, England one and France yet to get off the mark.

IRELAND: John Mattsson; Bertie O'Hanlon, William McKee, Patrick Reid, Barney Mullan; Jack Kyle, Hugh De Lacey; John Daly, Karl Mullen (Capt.), Albert McConnell, Colm Callan, Jimmy Nelson, Bill McKay, James McCarthy and Des O'Brien.

Ireland 6 Scotland 0
Lansdowne Road, February 28th, 1948

France's 11-3 defeat of Wales at Swansea the previous week dealt a serious blow to Wales' title ambitions leaving Ireland's nearest challengers a point behind but having played one game more. And so Ireland lined up at home for the first time in the campaign in rude health ready to face the challenge of Scotland.

Higgins was recalled at full-back and Michael O'Flanagan came into the centre for Reid. O'Flanagan, whose brother Kevin had played against Australia, was also a soccer international and, like his brother, a man of rounded sporting talents.

Ireland dismissed the Scottish threat with relative ease, running in two tries without reply, with Barney Mullan and Jack Kyle the men going over.

Incredibly, such had been the sequence of events in the series that Ireland's victory meant they had won the Championship with a game to spare, being three points ahead of Wales with just one game to play. The cherished prize of the Triple Crown, and one that had eluded Ireland for 49 years was now within touching distance.

IRELAND: Dudley Higgins; Bertie O'Hanlon, William McKee, Michael O'Flanagan, Barney Mullan; Jack Kyle, Hugh De Lacey; John Daly, Karl Mullen (Capt), Albert McConnell, Colm

Callan, Jimmy Nelson, Bill McKay, James McCarthy, Des O'Brien.

Ireland 6 Wales 3
Ravenhill, March 13th, 1948

As was the case in 2009 Ireland's last opponents was Wales. The showdown was scheduled for Belfast's Ravenhill for 13th March 1948.

Whereas in 2009 the populace was dealing with the fallout from the credit crunch, those immediate post war years were austere and sport provided a welcome diversion for people. And as in 2009, even those with little or no interest in rugby were captivated by the prospects that lay ahead.

Whereas France has so often proved to be Ireland's nemesis in the 21st Century, it was Wales who were Ireland's bogey team at that time. On no fewer than eight previous occasions they had foiled Ireland at the final hurdle, including the previous year in Swansea.

On the day, Ireland lined out with two changes. Reid was recalled at centre for O'Flanagan and Strathdee was back at scrum half.

The onslaught from the pack and the brilliance of Kyle gave Ireland the territorial advantage in the first half, which ended all square at 3-3. Barney Mullan's try for Ireland cancelled out by the great Wales centre Bleddyn Williams.

With the excitement at fever pitch among the 30,000 souls packed into Ravenhill, Ireland drew first blood early in the second half when Cobh man J.C. Daly got the vital score following a mistake by the Welsh full-back. The Irish pack drove forward with the energy and courage that had characterised their display all afternoon. Trott, the Welsh full-back, got to the ball but was unable to hold it and the irrepressible Daly was on hand to capitalise and send a nation into ecstasy. Sound familiar?

There would be no ninth slip-up on this occasion as Ireland kept their Celtic cousins at bay. With the forwards in command and Kyle to orchestrate the tactics behind the scrum, Ireland prevailed and a nation rejoiced.

Legend has it that Daly's shirt on the final whistle had been ripped from his back and cut up into a hundred pieces which were sold off as souvenirs.

In the remaining games England suffered defeats at Murrayfield 6-3, and in Paris 15-0 to end the campaign with the wooden spoon.

IRELAND: Dudley Higgins; Bertie O'Hanlon, William McKee, Patrick Reid, Barney Mullan; Jack Kyle, Ernie Strathdee, John Daly, Karl Mullen (Capt.), Albert McConnell, Colm Callan, Jimmy Nelson, Bill McKay, James McCarthy and Des O'Brien.

Never since that glorious day, until now has an Ireland side captured the Grand Slam and while many of those who fashioned that great achievement 61 years ago are playing now in the Elysian Fields, several of those distinguished men are still with us. Sadly the captain of the '48 team, Dr Karl Mullen died in his home in Kilcullen, Co Kildare, barely a month after being in Cardiff to see Brian O'Driscoll emulate his achievement in leading Ireland to a historic Grand Slam.

Using just 19 players, Ireland were champions and Triple Crown winners again in 1949 in what was only the fourth time that the Triple Crown had been retained by a home nation. Karl Mullen's men won their third Championship in four years in 1951. Halcyon days indeed. Over to you, Drico!

1948 Five Nations Championship

1st January 1948 to 29th March 1948

	Played	Won	Drew	Lost	Points For	Against	points +/-	Points
Ireland	4	4	0	0	36	16	20	8
France	4	2	0	2	40	25	15	4
Scotland	4	2	0	2	15	31	-16	4
Wales	4	1	1	2	23	20	3	3
England	4	0	1	3	16	35	-19	1

01/01/1948	France	6	Ireland	13	Stade Olympique de Colombes, Paris
17/01/1948	England	3	Wales	3	Twickenham, London
24/01/1948	Scotland	9	France	8	Murrayfield, Edinbrugh
07/02/1948	Wales	14	Scotland	0	National Stadium, Cardiff
14/02/1948	England	10	Ireland	11	Twickenham, London
14/02/1948	Wales	3	France	11	National Stadium, Cardiff
28/02/1948	Ireland	6	Scotland	0	Lansdowne Road, Dublin
13/03/1948	Ireland	6	Wales	3	Ravenhill, Belfast
20/03/1948	Scotland	6	England	3	Murrayfield, Edinbrugh
29/03/2010	France	15	England	0	Stade Olympique de Colombes, Paris

The Ireland Coaching Team

It would be unfair in a book dedicated to Ireland's 2009 success to ignore the role played by the previous manager, Eddie O'Sullivan. Since his appointment in November 2001, O'Sullivan transformed the fortunes of the Ireland team. He guided Ireland to 10 consecutive victories, a sequence that included some illustrious scalps such as Australia, England, France and Argentina. The run began with a 39-8 defeat of Romania in September 2002 and concluded with the Grand Slam decider defeat by England in March 2003.

Other landmarks in his career include securing Ireland a quarter-final place in the 2003 Rugby World Cup and so securing automatic qualification for the 2007 tournament.

Under his tutelage Ireland also beat the reigning 1999 World Champions, Australia; defeated reigning World Champions England in four successive RBS[1] Six Nations Championships, securing Ireland's first Triple Crown Championships in 19 years along the way in 2004. The wait for the next Triple Crown was somewhat shorter, coming a mere two years later in 2006. Another significant feather was added to the O'Sullivan cap when, in November 2004, Ireland defeated South Africa for the first time since 1965, running out 17-12 winners at Lansdowne Road.

However, O'Sullivan's failure to land the elusive RBS Six Nations Championship and to make any impact in the 2007 World Cup finally did for him.

---

[1] Royal Bank of Scotland

A fortnight before clinching his second Heineken Cup triumph with Munster, Declan Kidney was chosen by the powers that be in the IRFU to succeed O' Sullivan. Kidney was actually Ireland's assistant coach to Eddie O'Sullivan in 2002. The new man was charged with revitalising the fortunes of an Irish team that had slipped from the lofty heights of number two in the world rankings to a lowly eight. His contract will bring him at least to the World Cup in 2011 where it is hoped he will fare better than his predecessor who, although faced with the toughest group in the history of the competition, failed to unite the Irish camp and was accused of making some rather peculiar selection decisions. One of Declan Kidney's first tasks was to reunite the camp.

As a player, Kidney had a rather modest career, excelling at schools (PBC Cork[2]) and club level (Dolphin and UCC[3]) but never making it to international level. Nevertheless, it was as a coach that he showed more stunning potential. He returned to PBC as a coach and guided them to five junior cup wins in six years in the 1980s and three consecutive senior titles in the 1990s.

He led the Ireland Schools team to Triple Crown success in 1993 and then coached the Under 19s team that won the World Cup in 1998, before joining Munster where he played a major part in some of the greatest moments in Irish sport. After twice falling agonisingly short in the Heineken Cup (2000 and 2002) Kidney guided his men to remarkable victories in 2006 and 2008.

Kidney had a watching brief at Ireland's end-of-season tour of the Antipodes in 2008 and would have been encouraged by two gutsy and polished displays, where only fatigue after an exhausting season prevented Ireland from historic victories against the All Blacks and Wallabies.

A quiet and reserved man, Kidney's strength lies in his tactical awareness and the immense respect that his players have for him.

---

[2] Presentation Brothers College Cork
[3] University College Cork

Furthermore, the former schoolteacher is not afraid to delegate to specialist coaches. To that end he immediately assembled an impressive backroom team.

Backroom team

The former Springbok flanker, Gert Smal was appointed forwards coach, bringing a wealth of experience to the job. A man with an impressive CV of his own, he was assistant to Jake White in leading South Africa to glory in the World Cup in France in 2007 as well as the Tri Nations in 2004. He has also won two Currie Cups as a coach and coached the Stormers in Super 12.

Ireland's performances up front in the five games are a tribute, not alone to the players, but to the work of Smal.

Jamie Heaslip spoke of Smal's contribution to the Six Nations success:

"He's good. With regards to the rugby, he is intense. He is very, very detailed. With regards to lineouts, he does an unbelievable amount of work along with Paulie (O'Connell) and I think you can see that with the way we are defending lineouts.

"In open play he does a lot of continuity and rucking drills and most of the time you are seeing the offloading and reasonably quick, clean ball. He loves his scrums, loves his front five. Off the pitch we're trying to slag him about that punch he knocked out a Kiwi with, but he's not really taking to that too well."

In August 2008, Kidney made two further additions to his coaching team with the announcement that both Alan Gaffney and Mark Tainton would be joining the Ireland staff.

Both men are recognised as world class coaches in their respective fields and represented another significant capture for the Ireland team.

Gaffney was given the job of backs coach while holding on to his role in a similar capacity at Leinster. The ex-Bristol fly-half Tainton was retained as kicking coach.

Gaffney is a life member of the famous Randwick Rugby club in Sydney and has served as their coach since 1984. During that period, he held various roles including coach of the New South Wales Under 21s. At New South Wales Waratahs he was assistant to present Ulster coach Matt Williams (1997-99) from where he joined Leinster, again as assistant to Matt Williams. During that time, Leinster won the Celtic League in 2001/02 and were quarter-finalists in the Heineken Cup the same season.

With Declan Kidney moving on from Munster to Ireland in 2002, to become Eddie O'Sullivan's assistant, Gaffney took up the reins and in his three seasons with the province they won the Celtic League, Celtic Cup and were twice semi-finalists in the Heineken Cup. In the summer of 2005, he took the position of backs coach of Australia, leaving them in 2005 to coach Saracens in the Guinness Premiership and leading them to the semi-final of the Heineken Cup where they ironically almost beat Munster.

Mark Tainton was capped at both England A and U23 levels in his career, during which he scored over 3,000 points.

After his retirement from competitive rugby in 1997, he was appointed kicking coach for the England tour to Argentina that summer. He moved further into coaching and was head coach for Richmond Rugby in the English Premiership from 1997-1999.

Following that, he was appointed Director of Rugby for Oxford University from 1999-2002, winning three varsity games.

Throughout his coaching career he continued to deliver his considerable kicking expertise on a consultancy basis and began working with Munster in 2002, following which he joined the Ireland squad and worked with them until the end of the 2008 RBS Six Nations Championship.

Commenting on the announcement Declan Kidney said, "We are delighted to have both Alan and Mark on board with Ireland. Both of them are extremely strong technical coaches in their areas and so I think they will bring a further positive mix to the coaching team and squad."

Forty-five-year-old Less Kiss was appointed Defence Coach. Highly rated in his native Australia, he moved from wing with the Kangaroos team of 1986, who played rugby league of a very high standard, to union, coaching with the Springboks; three South African Super 14 sides (the Stormers, Cats and Bulls) and latterly in Sydney with the Watatahs; Kiss has a broad knowledge base.

Ireland rookie Luke Fitzgerald was gushing in his praise of the man's contribution to the rise of Irish rugby: "I think he's fantastic. He's brought so much to the set-up. Defence is his main area and he's been brilliant for us there.

"He has an awful lot of new ideas and new thoughts on how to stop teams breaking us down and he actually has a few interesting things to say in terms of attack as well."

Former Ireland international winger Paul McNaughton, who was honoured 15 times by Ireland in the '70s and '80s, was given the role of Manager. His position as Leinster manager was followed by his appointment to their Provincial Management Committee. Pragmatic and efficient, his straight dealing is said to be his greatest asset.

THE 2009 SQUAD

Declan Kidney initially announced a 39-man squad for the 2009 RBS Six Nations Championship.

The squad included a number of uncapped players, including Cian Healy and Ryan Caldwell, with Ulster centre Darren Cave making his first appearance in a senior Ireland squad.

The panel also included Leinster's Gordon D'Arcy, who had made a recent welcome return for the province following a long term arm injury.

Leo Cullen, Tony Buckley, Neil Best and Roger Wilson were not considered for inclusion in the senior squad due to either injury or suspension.

The large squad size allowed any overseas-based (especially Guinness Premiership players) the opportunity to return to their clubs on the Wednesday of the first week.

Kidney said: "We want to continue to develop a panel and bringing in 39 players allows to us to work with the players on this basis.

"As well as bringing the players through the systems of the team, it allows for the usual knocks the players might pick up.

"The core group of players who were part of the November 2008 squad have maintained their form but it is also pleasing to be able to bring in players who are really developing this season, like Darren Cave and Tom Court, as well as more established players who have performed well over the last number of weeks."

A nine-man 'A' team panel of players was also selected. It included Ulster's Ian Humphreys, Leinster back rower Sean O'Brien and Connacht's Sean Cronin.

Speaking about the Championship, the Irish coach added: 'The RBS Six Nations is one of, if not the best annual international tournaments in the world and a great sporting occasion in Ireland.

'The Guinness Series in November was mission accomplished from a rankings point of view and the win against Argentina [a 17-3 success at Croke Park in November 2008], although not the prettiest game anybody may have seen, was vitally important.'

IRELAND SQUAD – 2009
RBS Six NATIONS CHAMPIONSHIP:

Backs

Tommy Bowe (Ospreys)

Ian Dowling (Shannon – Munster)*

Girvan Dempsey (Terenure College – Leinster)

Darren Cave (Belfast Harlequins – Ulster)*

Gordon D'Arcy (Lansdowne – Leinster)

Keith Earls (Young Munster – Munster)

Luke Fitzgerald (Blackrock College – Leinster)

Shane Horgan (Boyne – Leinster)

Robert Kearney (UCD – Leinster)

Geordan Murphy (Leicester)

Brian O'Driscoll (UCD – Leinster)

Ronan O'Gara (Cork Constitution – Munster)

Tomas O'Leary (Dolphin – Munster)

Eoin Reddan (Wasps)

Jonathan Sexton (St. Mary's College – Leinster)*

Peter Stringer (Shannon – Munster)

Andrew Trimble (Ballymena – Ulster)

Paddy Wallace (Ballymena – Ulster)

Forwards

Rory Best (Banbridge – Ulster)

Ryan Caldwell (Dungannon – Ulster)*

Bob Casey (London Irish)

Tom Court (Malone – Ulster)*

Stephen Ferris (Dungannon – Ulster)

Jerry Flannery (Shannon – Munster)

John Hayes (Bruff – Munster)

Cian Healy (Clontarf – Leinster)*

Jamie Heaslip (Naas – Leinster)

Marcus Horan (Shannon – Munster)

Bernard Jackman (Clontarf – Leinster)

Shane Jennings (St. Mary's College – Leinster)

Denis Leamy (Cork Constitution – Munster)

Donncha O'Callaghan (Cork Constitution – Munster)

Paul O'Connell (Young Munster – Munster)

Mick O'Driscoll (Cork Constitution – Munster)

Malcolm O'Kelly (St. Mary's College – Leinster)

Alan Quinlan (Shannon – Munster)

Mike Ross (Harlequins)*

Donnacha Ryan (Shannon - Munster)

David Wallace (Garryowen - Munster)

* Uncapped players

Note: The squad was eventually reduced to 27 players. It is the biographies of those 27 that follow.

The Backs

Tommy Bowe

Born:	**Craigavon, 22nd February 1984**
Height:	**1.91m/ 6' 3"**
Weight:	**96kg/15st 2lbs**
Position:	**Universal Back**
Club:	**Ospreys**
Debut for Ireland:	**vs USA November 2004**

A consistent try scorer for Ulster in the Magners League and Heineken Cup, until his move to the Cardiff Ospreys in the summer of 2008, Tommy Bowe scored 10 tries in 23 Test matches, opening his account on his debut in the 55-6 demolition of the USA in November 2004 and reaching double figures with the crucial score in the 2009 Championship decider in the Millennium Stadium.

Bowe played in every minute of every game in the successful 2009 campaign. That said, it hasn't been all plain sailing for the former Monaghan minor Gaelic footballer, who became the first man from the Farney County to play for Ireland in 80 years when he lined out against the US Eagles, now managed, ironically, by one Eddie O'Sullivan.

From thereon, however, he struggled to get further Test experience due to dips in form, injury and with Dennis Hickie, Shane Horgan and Girvan Dempsey blocking his path. His Test career may also have suffered from playing on the left, and not his preferred right wing.

A star performer at underage international level, he was injured for Ireland's defeat by New Zealand Colts in the 2003 Under-21 World Cup final.

While missing the entire 2005 Six Nations campaign, the Ulster flyer returned to play in seven matches in a row for Ireland before once again losing his place.

Bowe was dropped for the 2006 RBS Six Nations clash with Wales following a dip in form. His then Ulster team-mate, Andrew Trimble, replaced him, making the left-wing spot his own for a period.

He returned for the summer tour to Argentina in 2007 but was unavailable for the autumn internationals with a hamstring injury and also missed out on the 2008 World Cup.

The move to Ospreys reignited Bowe's career. The sturdy winger who can also play at centre, made his Magners League debut for Ospreys against Connacht in September 2008.

In an interesting selection, Bowe was named on the Ospreys left wing ahead of the mercurial Welsh international star Shane Williams, who remained on the bench.

On the international front, he came back with a bang in the 2008 Six Nations when he touched down twice against Scotland. Subsequent starts against Wales, England, New Zealand and Australia saw him emerge as one of Ireland's most consistent performers in 2008.

Those performances earned him a place in the back line for the RBS Six Nations opener against France in 2009 where he didn't disappoint. Ever on the lookout for a burst, it was his surge that led to the vital confidence boosting opening try for Jamie Heaslip. He went one better in the second Test against Italy getting himself on the score sheet for Ireland's opening try against the Azzurri. His great anticipation and sharpness for the intercept was a classic piece of wing play that turned the afternoon in Ireland's favour.

Not surprisingly he was retained for the clash with England and was only denied a try by Mark Cueto who just beat him to a fingertip touchdown.

Against Scotland he continued to deploy his footballing nous to good effect, coming in off the wing when the side lacked cohesion. His superlative tackle, on the half time whistle was arguably the game's turning point.

Tommy Bowe sealed his place in Irish sporting history with a scoring display against Wales that highlighted a memorable Six Nations campaign. Biting the hand that feeds him, he took Ireland's decisive try splendidly and could easily have scored another to set up Ireland for a grandstand finish and that elusive Grand Slam. One of the finds of the season, Bowe was rewarded with a call up to the Lions' squad.

Girvan Dempsey

Born:	**Dublin, 2nd October 1975**
Height:	**1.83 m/6'2"**
Weight:	**91kgs/14st 4lbs**
Position:	**Full Back/Winger**
Province:	**Leinster**
Club:	**Terenure College**
Debut for Ireland:	**vs Georgia, Nov 1998**

Girvan Dempsey will probably be best remembered for his memorable try in the left corner against England at Twickenham in 2004, a score that built the platform for a historic Triple Crown triumph. Ireland's first since 1985.

An excellent reader of the game who consistently impresses in defence and attack, Dempsey won his first full cap as a replacement for Conor O'Shea in the 70-0 thrashing of Georgia in November 1998. He marked the occasion with a brace of tries. Ironically the last of his 19 tries (which makes him fourth in the list of top Irish try scorers) also came in a defeat of Georgia. That victory was much less straightforward with Ireland running out marginal winners 14-10 in the 2007 World Cup Group game.

Dempsey became a regular in the side after coming on against England in February 2000 and since then he has been almost ever-present when fit, and played in all five of Ireland's matches at the 2003 World Cup but thereafter became locked in a fierce battle with Geordan Murphy for the full-back duties.

He appeared in 29 consecutive Tests from 2003-05 and nine times as a wing in 1998-99 despite his career being predominantly as a full back, a position from which he scored 12 of his international tries.

He was ever-present during Ireland's Triple Crown-winning run in the 2007 Six Nations – he scored three tries against England

and two against Italy and reached a milestone when winning his 50th cap in the 2004 summer tour's second Test against South Africa.

Dempsey may be less naturally gifted than his friend and rival, but is no slouch in attack. The Leinster three-quarter is a safer option for the Number 15 jersey, solid under the high ball and strong in defence. But Ireland's expansive style restricted his opportunities over the 2009 Six Nations campaign, as he is the most limited of a world-class back-line.

Educated at Terenure College and the National College of Ireland, Dempsey is a former Ireland Under 21 and 'A' cap. He made his Leinster debut in 1996.

A seasoned campaigner, Dempsey is the fifth most capped Irish international with 82 Test appearances to his name. He provides excellent cover at wing and full back from the bench and is strong in defence but has little chance of winning a place in the starting line-up if everyone is fit, as was the case for the 2009 RBS Six Nations. Although named among the reduced 27 man squad the 33 year old failed to make it to the bench.

Gordon D'Arcy

Born:	**Wexford, 10th February 1980**
Height:	**1.80m/5' 11"**
Weight:	**90kgs/14st 2bs**
Position:	**Centre/ Full Back/Winger**
Province:	**Leinster**
Club:	**Lansdowne**
Debut for Ireland:	**vs Romania October 1999**

When Gordon D'Arcy was called up by former Ireland supremo Warren Gatland to tour with the full Ireland side, he replied: "thanks but no thanks, I've got too much homework"! Typical teenager.

A colossus despite his smallish build, D'Arcy was the Six Nations Player of the Year in 2004, but dogged by hamstring and back injuries he has failed to scale those heights since.

Educated at Clongowes Wood College, D'Arcy helped his school win the Leinster Senior Cup in 1998. Capped for Ireland at Schools, Under 19, and Under 21 level, he put in a fine performance on his Ireland 'A' debut against France at Donnybrook in November 1999.

A dip in form saw him lose his place with Leinster and subsequently at senior international level. However, he returned to play at Under 21 international level in games against Scotland, Italy, France and Wales. The hard-running youngster was then fast-tracked into the senior squad when injury forced Girvan Dempsey to withdraw and he made his debut as a replacement for Conor O'Shea in a pool game against Romania at the 1999 Rugby World Cup. He was to wait another three years for his second cap.

Back to full fitness, a number of eye-catching displays for Leinster saw D'Arcy gain an international recall for the start of the

2004 RBS Six Nations, ironically coming into the Ireland starting line-up for his injured provincial colleague Brian O'Driscoll.

Making up for lost time, D'Arcy was superb during the tournament with his first two Test tries helping Ireland to a 37-16 Triple Crown-clinching win over Scotland. He was named the BBC Player of the RBS Six Nations that year.

A dynamic centre with lightning quick feet and an enviable rugby brain, D'Arcy became part of arguably the best centre partnership in the world alongside Brian O'Driscoll. He made the Number 12 position his own for three seasons, playing in all 19 of Ireland's Test matches between November 2005 and March 2007.

He had missed virtually all of the 2005 RBS Six Nations with a hamstring injury, before making a comeback in time for the Lions tour to New Zealand in 2005 illustrating how far he had come since his first training match for Wexford Wanderers Under 12s.

Slowly he recovered his form and, by that year's November internationals, was close to his explosive best. An agile ball-carrier with dazzling footwork, D'Arcy may be short for a modern centre, but is tenacious and deceptively powerful in attack and defence.

In 2006/2007 D'Arcy was one of Ireland's most effective players and was voted player of the 2007 Championship by fans on Irish Rugby.ie.

Hampered by injury, he suffered a broken arm against Italy in February 2008, he was then sidelined for the remainder of that year's Championship. D'Arcy sustained the blow when tackling Italian out-half Andrea Masi in the 26th minute of the Championship opener in Dublin. It was desperate luck for the Leinster centre who was hoping to hit the ground running in the Championship and show the sort of form which won him the Six Nations Player of the Tournament in 2004.

D'Arcy marked a stunning return to international action in the 2009 RBS Six Nations opener against France. A 29th minute replacement for Paddy Wallace, his match-securing try in the 30-21 victory led to calls for the Wexford man to renew his midfield partnership with O'Driscoll for the round two game against Italy.

Considering his difficult rehabilitation after his arm break, D'Arcy's eye-catching cameo was hugely encouraging for Ireland coach Declan Kidney. That said, Kidney stuck with the man in possession and once again it was Wallace who started, albeit being replaced by the ever improving D'Arcy in the second half.

He wasn't used against England but replaced Wallace in the starting line up against Scotland for his first start in over a year. He showed enough to retain his place for the showdown against Wales. Winning his 41st cap, his consistent contribution helped Ireland sink the defending Six Nations champions.

D'Arcy capped the best season of his career thus far with a winners' medal following Leinster's defeat of Leicester Tigers in the 2009 Heineken Cup final.

He probably thought his season had ended following that win at Murrayfield but was called up to join the Lions in South Africa because of injury concerns in the back division.

Lions' coach Ian McGeechan in justifying the late call up said: "Gordon's partnership with Brian O'Driscoll is a proven one and can only benefit the Lions' squad here in South Africa.

"Gordon showed in the European Cup final and the recent Barbarians match against England (when they won 33-26) that he is back to his best.

"He was on our reserve list and we had no hesitation in calling him up to the squad as he is an extremely experienced player who has played 41 times for his country."

Keith Earls

Born:	**Moyross, 2nd October 1987**
Height:	**1.8m/5'11"**
Weight:	**90kg/14st 2lbs**
Position:	**Universal Back**
Province:	**Munster**
Club:	**Young Munster**
Debut for Ireland:	**vs Canada, November 2008**

The Young Munster clubman is one of the most exciting young talents in Irish rugby and has a bright future ahead of him. Injury kept him out of the beginning of the 2009 Six Nations but by the second week he was fully fit and back in training eagerly awaiting the challenges that lay ahead.

Keith Earls was educated at St Munchin's College in Limerick City. He represented the college at all levels, culminating in a Munster Schools Senior Cup winners' medal in 2006, where he scored tries in every round including the winner in the final against PBC Cork on St. Patrick's Day.

One of several sons of famous fathers in the Ireland squad, the 21-year-old from Limerick, is the son of Young Munster legend Ger Earls. An all-action full-back or centre with bags of pace, Earls followed in his father's footsteps to Young Munster.

He was a member of the 2007 Grand Slam-winning Under 20s side and has also been capped for Ireland A, scoring in each of the Ireland 'A' team's matches at the 2007 Churchill Cup. He has also represented his country's Sevens side.

Earls progressed through the ranks at Munster at a rate of knots. Blistering performances in the AIB[4] League and some huge

---

[4] Allied Irish Bank

games for Munster in the Magners League and in the Heineken Cup saw him catapulted into the senior side.

He made his debut in the 55-0 destruction of Canada at Thomond Park in the neighbouring parish to where he grew up. There was a mere two minutes and 27 seconds on the stadium clock when he broke the tackle of Mike Burak to crash over for the first of Ireland's eight tries.

The explosive arrival of Earls into the Ireland team gave veteran Munster and Ireland flanker Alan Quinlan particular reason to feel every one of his 34 years.

"I feel like an old man – I played with his dad and against him for years, and it's kind of strange playing with Keith now," he admitted.

"He's a very exciting prospect but the key for Keith is that he's a very balanced young lad and keeps his feet on the ground. He's willing to work really hard and has a great attitude about him.

"He's not going to get excited. It's obviously extra special for him to score on his debut, but he has a great work ethic, he's a great player with a massive future."

Earls won his second cap against New Zealand a week later in 3-22 defeat at Croke Park.

A Magners league winner with Munster in 2009, Earls was named in the 2009 Lions squad for the tour to South Africa, despite not managing any pitch time in the 2009 RBS Six Nations.

Luke Fitzgerald

Born:	Dublin, 13th September 1987
Height:	1.86m/ 6'1"
Weight:	92 kg/14st 7lbs
Position:	Full Back/Winger
Club:	Blackrock College/Leinster
Province:	Leinster
Debut for Ireland:	vs Pacific Islands, November 2006

"He's fast, his work ethic is excellent and he's got beautiful balance. He has that fantastic ability to make defenders look absolutely stupid."

At 19 years and two months, Luke Fitzgerald became the youngest player to play for Ireland since Alistair McGibbin against Wales in 1977, when he lined up in the back line for the demolition of the Pacific Islanders in November 2006. He achieved another landmark of sorts that day by becoming the 999th player to be capped by Ireland.

Comfortable at full-back, on the wing or at centre, Fitzgerald was capped by the Leinster and Ireland Schools teams and was part of the Ireland Schools XV that completed a clean sweep of wins in 2005. He capped that memorable season by winning the Irish Examiner Young Rugby Player of the Year award.

Unsurprisingly he was on the Irish rugby authority's radar as a player to watch from an early age and his rise to the senior scene has been nothing short of meteoric. Just six months prior to his senior call up he had been playing schools rugby, driving Blackrock College to a 65th Schools Cup final win against St Michael's College in 2006. He had just completed his Leaving Cert that summer and in September he lined out for Leinster for the first time. Breaking into Leinster's back-line was an achievement in itself, and it was his form with them, which included tries on his Heineken Cup debut against Edinburgh as well as a stand out performance on his 'A' international debut against Australia 'A' that saw him catapulted into the senior side.

Since then, the rookie with the excellent hands and the vision to unlock defences has been outfoxing defences in the Magners League and Heineken Cup, chiselling out a fine early career with province and country.

A talent-laden back with an enviable box of tricks, Fitzgerald comes from a strong rugby pedigree with his father being former Ireland prop Des Fitzgerald who won 34 Ireland caps between 1984 and 1992.

Selected on the left wing for the opening game of the 2009 RBS Six Nations against France, the youngster never took a backward step and with 13 tackles actually ended the contest at the apex of the tacklers count. He capped that performance with a Man of the Match display in the Battle of Rome, running superb angles, defending strongly and notching up a brace of tries for good measure, his first for his country.

With each successive game Fitzgerald's growing maturity became more evident. And when opportunities were limited as was the case in the Tests against England, Scotland and Wales, the youngster went about his basic chores in an efficient and workmanlike manner.

A key component in Ireland's success he won his 12th cap in the showdown at the Millennium Stadium and was named in the Lions' squad for 2009. If that wasn't enough he collected a Heineken Cup winners' medal just weeks after the Grand Slam success when Leinster defeated Leicester in the final at Murrayfield. As his former Ireland coach Eddie O'Sullivan said: "He's the full bag of chips!"

Shane Horgan

Born:	**Bellewstown, Co Meath, 18th July 1978**
Height:	**1.93cm/6'4"**
Weight:	**104kgs/16st 5bs**
Position:	**Winger/Centre**
Club:	**Lansdowne**
Province:	**Leinster**
Debut for Ireland:	**vs Scotland, Feb 2000**

Arguably Shane Horgan's best moment in an Ireland shirt was his try in the 24-28 defeat of England at Twickenham in 2006 that won the match and the Triple Crown for Ireland. In a stunning finish, he displayed the strength to absorb a desperate tackle by England's Lewis Moody in the corner and the dexterity to reach way out in front to touch the ball down with his outstretched fingertips. It was a splendid finish to a memorable movement and gave Ireland the victory they deserved. It was Horgan's second try of the game. England in defeat shipped a record number of points against Ireland (28) in what was Ireland's third consecutive victory over the English. For his exertions, Horgan, nicknamed Shaggy, was named in the RBS Dream Team of that 2006 Championship.

His run of four tries in seven outings in that campaign and in the 2007 Triple Crown success, which again included an unforgettable cross-field catch and touchdown in the 2007 Croke Park encounter with England, rubber-stamped Horgan's reputation as a top quality wide man.

One of the most dangerous strike runners in Test rugby, he is equally at home on the wing or at centre. The Leinster back had been Ireland's first choice for the Number 14 jersey, but his roaming role – he frequently comes off the wing and bursts through the midfield – has proved highly effective. Horgan is fast and powerful, but is far more than a simple battering ram, thanks to excellent handling and vision.

In November 1996 he made his Ireland Youths debut against Spain. In all he played five times at that level and in February '98 he made his Ireland Under 21 debut against Scotland and also played at that level against England, Wales and France.

A powerfully-built winger who has developed into a world class finisher, Shaggy cemented his place on Ireland's right wing after winning his first cap against Scotland in February 2000 and he marked the occasion by scoring his first international try. Ronan O'Gara, Simon Easterby and Peter Stringer also made their full international debuts that day.

In 2002 Horgan was dogged by injuries but returned to play a full part in the 2003 Rugby World Cup and was ever-present in Ireland's Triple Crown-winning team the following year.

Never given a start during the Lions tour of New Zealand in 2005, he came on as a replacement for each of the Test matches.

He marked the occasion of his 50th cap for Ireland against Australia in November 2006, with his 17th international try.

A knee injury hampered his build-up to the 2007 Rugby World Cup but he regained full fitness and toured New Zealand and Australia in June 2008, starting both games.

Born in Drogheda and educated at St. Mary's, Drogheda, Horgan has had a stop-start career ravaged by injury. The former Meath minor Gaelic footballer has played a total of 64 games for Ireland, mostly on the wing but quite often as a centre. Named in the squad for the 2009 campaign, he didn't make the pitch. His disappointment may have been eased slightly by picking up a Heineken Cup winners' medal with Leinster a mere six weeks after the Slam.

Horgan won his last cap in the 55-0 defeat of Canada in November 2008. He has amassed 20 tries along the way making him Ireland's third all-time try scorer.

Rob Kearney

Born:	**Louth, 26th March 1986**
Height:	**1.85cm/6'1"**
Weight:	**90kg/14st 2lbs**
Position:	**Wing/Full back**
Club:	**UCD**
Province:	**Leinster**
Debut for Ireland:	**vs Argentina, June 2007**

At the time of the 2007 RBS Six Nations Championship, Rob Kearney was a mere squad member. But by the time Declan Kidney named his maiden Six Nations team in 2009, Kearney had leapfrogged several other players, who had previously been ahead of him in the pecking order, to secure the Number 15 jersey.

Rock solid under the high ball and lightning quick in attack, Kearney became a regular in the Ireland team after impressing as a replacement against Italy in the opening tie of the 2008 Championship.

He put in several more eye-catching performances in that Championship, scoring tries against Scotland and England. That, allied to his performances on the summer 2008 tour to New Zealand and South Africa, in which he was widely acknowledged as Ireland's best player, helped establish him as a senior international.

Kearney, who is used by Leinster at full-back and on the wing, first came to prominence at Schools level with Clongowes Wood. His Leinster debut followed in 2005 and Irish caps at Under 19 and 'A' levels came before his senior debut in a 16-0 reverse against Argentina in June 2007.

In the first game of 2009 RBS Six Nations against France the 24-year-old vindicated the clamour for him to play at full back. He did enough to make the berth his own for the Championship.

A rude awakening was in store in the next Test against Italy, when in the first minute he was the victim of a dangerously high tackle by Andrea Masi, although he still managed to hold on to the ball. Masi, in addition to a well deserved yellow card, was handed a three-week ban.

Unperturbed by the violent attack, Kearney went on to put in another stand-out performance, combining great counter-attacking with responsibility under high ball.

Against England he laid down another marker for a Lions spot and looked an accomplished player through and through.

He followed up with a couple of dependable displays in the games against Scotland and Wales. In the latter, when winning his 16th cap he was, considering his tender years, incredibly cool and resourceful and calmed any number of Irish nerves.

Kearney, whose younger brother David played for the Irish Under 20s in 2008, and could well follow in his brother's footsteps, is thriving under the new regime and developed into a truly world class player over the course of the Six Nations campaign. A Heineken Cup winner's medal with Leinster was added to his growing collection of medals soon after the Slam was claimed and, not surprisingly he was rewarded with a place on the Lions tour to South Africa.

Geordan Murphy

Born: Naas, 19th April 1978
Position: Winger/Full Back
Height: 183cms/6'1"
Weight: 97kgs/15st 3lbs
Club: Leicester Tigers
Debut for Ireland: vs USA, June 2000

One of the most naturally talented back-line players Ireland has produced in the modern era, Geordan Murphy has shown his versatility by playing on both wings, at full-back and centre for his country and he actually stepped in as a replacement out-half on a tour to Argentina in 2007.

The only English based player in Ireland's 2009 Six Nations squad, Murphy was educated at Newbridge College, helping his school reach the 1995/96 Leinster Senior Cup final which they lost to Blackrock. He is the youngest of six children all of whom played rugby union.

He had a six-month spell at Auckland Grammar School in New Zealand on a rugby exchange and whilst studying at Waterford Institute of Technology, the Kildare man had a dual role with Naas and Waterpark.

In September 1997, as a callow 19-year-old he crossed the channel to join Leicester Tigers. He arrived at Leicester, then in the hands of the legendary Australian coach Bob Dwyer for a three week trial as a mere cub hoping to realise his dream.

Following his switch to Leicester, Murphy made steady progress to the Irish Under 21, 'A' and senior squads, having already been honoured at Under 19 level.

During the 1998/99 season he made his Ireland Under 21 debut against France and in March 2000 he was called into the Ireland squad to win his first 'A' cap against Italy.

In his time with the English heavyweights, Murphy has picked up numerous honours – the Tigers were League Champions five times between 1999 and 2007 – the EDF Energy Cup was secured in 2007 and two Heineken Cups, in 2001and 2002 were added to Murphy's burgeoning collection of medals. He actually scored a try in the 2002 final win over Munster.

Murphy's history with Ireland has never been straightforward. He came into the Ireland side in the summer of 2000 against a backdrop of sustained bewilderment in Leicester that their jewel had not already been crowned by his country. The standard response from the then Irish coaching team of Warren Gatland and Eddie O'Sullivan was that he needed to be the regular full-back for Leicester (where Tim Stimpson was the last line of defence with Murphy on the wing), before he could claim a starting spot for Ireland.

That summer, against the USA in New Hampshire, in sweltering heat and against hapless opponents, Ireland racked up 83 points. Murphy picked up two tries and all seemed well enough. By the autumn, however, things had cooled substantially and a drop in form saw him back in the Ireland 'A' team and he didn't play for the senior side again until the following summer.

In the opening game of the 2002 Six Nations he scored two tries in Ireland's record 54-10 victory over Wales at Lansdowne Road. He retained his place for the game against England but was forced to retire injured in the opening minutes.

He began the 2003 season on the bench before gaining a regular place in the starting line-up for the rest of the championship.

In the absence of Brian O'Driscoll, he played in the unfamiliar role of outside centre in the June 2003 Test against Australia in Perth and looked set to scale the heights at the 2003 Rugby World Cup but a cruel leg break in a warm up game against Scotland saw him sidelined.

He returned with vigour to score in the 2004 Triple Crown-clinching win over the Scots. A Test cap for the Lions against New Zealand followed and he played in 10 of Ireland's Tests in 2006, adding another Triple Crown. A third Triple Crown was added in 2007 and once again he was ever-present in the campaign. Thereafter, however, while his club career was flourishing a loss of form and the resurgence of Leinster full-back Girvan Dempsey contributed to him losing his place in the Irish team.

In Murphy, Ireland boast a playmaking full back who is arguably the envy of every other home nation and he has an impressive fan club. Dubbed the "George Best of Rugby" by former Leicester boss Dean Richards; Martin Johnson described him as the slickest retriever of the ball in the business, while his Ireland captain Brian O'Driscoll has described him as the most talented player he has seen in training. Former England captain Martin Corry named him as full-back in his dream XV from those he has played for and against: "Proof that skinny men can play rugby. One of those quality players you line up against and think 'Shit, I wish he was on my team! He seems to have patented the chewing gum tackle and has no fear of clinging on to your ankles until you come down."

That said, however, the man himself is often quizzed about the split in his personality between club and country:

"I get asked all the time, I can't put my finger on it. It's frustrating because people say: 'What is it?' I'm not doing anything differently. I'm eating the same things; I'm wearing the same boots.

"Obviously things are a little different with Leicester; moves are called around me and the pattern of play is a little different." Murphy is adamant that no matter what anyone says he wants to win with Ireland as much as he does for his club.

Murphy is a fabulously-gifted player, with rare vision, but has been plagued by inconsistency at Test level. Indeed watching him play can be a frustrating experience: the Tigers three quarter can be error-prone, often at considerable cost – as in Paris in 2006, when his mistakes handed France two tries. Having initially battled with Girvan Dempsey for the full-back duties his battle is now with Rob Kearney.

And by the time of the 2009 Six Nations Kearney was the man in possession. Murphy managed just four minutes of the opener against France winning his 60th cap. He wasn't used against England or Italy and took over from Kearney late in the second half in the games against Scotland and Wales to take his caps tally to 62, during which time he has notched up 18 tries.

Brian O'Driscoll

Born:	**Dublin, 21st January 1979**
Height:	**1.75m/5'9"**
Weight:	**95kgs/15st**
Position:	**Centre**
Province:	**Leinster**
Club:	**Blackrock College**
Debut for Ireland:	**vs Australia, June 1999**

"If only Achilles had his heel. Brian O'Driscoll is the player without weakness or flaw. A lethal finisher, a lion in defence, a brilliant leader, he is the greatest rugby player on earth."

Jeremy Guscott was one of the most celebrated centres of all time, a sorcerer for England and the Lions, yet even at his peak he feels he would have trailed O'Driscoll by the length of a field:

"It takes an awful lot for me to be lost for words, but there are times when I've watched Brian play when I find it is difficult to find words to sum him up. He's easily the best centre in the world."

Former England captain Martin Corry named him as full-back in his dream XV from those he has played for and against: "The complete player, who combines powerful attacking abilities with a strong defensive base."

Although those who remember Mike Gibson, Ollie Campbell or Jack Kyle may protest, O'Driscoll is the outstanding Irish rugby player of all time. His body of work, his portfolio of achievement, his lack of any obvious weakness, his insistence on seeing only possibilities where others view obstacles puts O'Driscoll, even among the greats, in a league of his own.

It is difficult to know where to start with a man whose CV boasts Ireland's record try scorer; a Triple Crown winner four times; World Player of the Year nominee; Lions captain – and the list goes on, but that tells only the bones of the story of a man who is worthy of a volume of books on his own.

The Dublin born star was educated at Blackrock College and University College Dublin. In 1996 he made his debut for Ireland Schools and in 1998 won the FIRA Under 19 World Youth Championship under the tutelage of current Ireland coach Declan Kidney.

In February 1999 he made his Ireland Under 21 debut against France. He won his first cap playing against Australia in the summer tour of 1999. During the 1999/00 season he played a part in all four of Ireland's Rugby World Cup games, scoring his first international try in the 53-8 defeat of the United States.

O'Driscoll first made global headlines when a stunning hat-trick of tries against France in 2000 lit up that year's Five Nations and helped Ireland to their first win in Paris for 28 years. Another brilliant hat-trick followed against Scotland in the 2002 competition as did a nomination for the 2002 IRB[5] World Player of the Year award.

Yet another hat-trick followed in Ireland's opening game (v Divisional XV) of their 2002 summer tour of New Zealand; dropped goals in both Tests v the All Blacks were the icing on the cake.

In the summer of 2001 he played in all three Tests for the Lions against Australia. The first test produced the defining moment of Brian's career. Australia pride themselves on their defence, but during that tour, the Dubliner found the holes and a magnificent try awoke the rest of the world to his unique gifts.

He captained Ireland for the first time when winning his 31st cap in the 18-9 Irish victory against Australia in November 2002, and took over the captaincy on a permanent basis for the 2004 RBS Six Nations.

---

[5] International Rugby Board

His Leinster team-mate, Gordon D'Arcy's return to the Ireland side that year saw the pair strike up a fine midfield partnership at Test level. The fleet-footed duo, acting as both swords and shields, played key roles in the recent successes of province and country. As well as the Ireland trophy haul, Leinster lifted the Magners League trophy in 2008 and the Heineken Cup in 2009.

In 2005, he became Ireland's first Lions captain since Ciaran Fitzgerald in 1983. He never got the chance to underline his status as one of the world's best centres, however, being the victim of the most infamous off the ball incident in rugby history. The spear tackle by Tama Umaga and Kevin Mealamu in the first Test kept him out of the game for six months.

He returned to full fitness to lead Ireland to Triple Crown triumphs in 2006 and 2007 and to the Grand Slam in 2009 and was named as the RBS Player of the Six Nations in each year.

Brian's first visit to Twickenham with Ireland in March 2003 ended in a 50-18 defeat and although the 21-year-old did manage one special moment, retrieving his own chip during the second half, the response of TV commentator Stuart Barnes that "how O'Driscoll must wish he was wearing the white of England" must have made him cringe.

English commentators throughout the ages have made similar comments about other top Irish sportsmen, most notably about George Best. Why they think any self-respecting proud Irishman would want to wear anything but a green jersey never mind the white of an England team displays their total ignorance of the Irish psyche.

Our man had his revenge in spades, however, and achieved everlasting unpopularity (at Twickenham only), as Ireland prepared to meet the newly crowned World Champions in the first post-World Cup match in 2003. He characterised their fans as corporate swillers whom he hoped would choke on their prawn sandwiches when Ireland put them to the sword in their own back yard. His saving grace was the fact that Ireland did exactly that, winning 19-13.

O'Driscoll, who retained the captaincy under the new Kidney regime, may have been eclipsed by the dazzling progress of some of his team-mates at times in recent years; he nevertheless remains as influential and dangerous as ever. Thus far he has led Ireland a record 63 times in 93 Test matches culminating in success in the 2009 Six Nations Championship.

The talisman of a squad straining against the leash of history, the team is shaped in his image. His gladiatorial spirit has elevated other Irishmen to great heights. O'Driscoll combines sheer determination, brilliant defensive qualities, dazzling attacking skills and a winning mentality to be one of the most feared players in the world.

His prominent role in the opening game against France was capped by a superb intercept try early in the second half. His reputation precedes him, however, with opposition teams shutting him down quickly, giving him less space to work in, but this has the positive effect of creating opportunities for those around him. He is blessed with vision, handling, speed and strength that enable him to blast through gaps or create openings. While Italy shut down the wide channels very effectively, O'Driscoll still managed a few trademark interventions, including that try, and defended with his usual awareness and aggression.

Against Scotland it was his defensive abilities that were on show as Ireland found themselves under the cosh in the first half. In the second period the captain popped up to score a vital try, joining the forwards in a ruck to force his way over.

His try against Wales in the final game was his fourth of the competition and his 36th for Ireland. It also made him the 2009 competition's top try scorer alongside England's Flutely. The 2009 Six Nations' Player of the Tournament now stands alone as Ireland's top try scorer.

Ronan O'Gara

Born:	San Diego, 7th March 1977
Position:	Fly half
Height:	18.3m/6'0"
Weight:	83kgs/13st 0lbs
Club:	Cork Constitution
Province:	Munster
Debut for Ireland:	vs Scotland, February 2000

Ronan O'Gara has been the catalyst for Ireland's transformation from World Cup also rans to Grand Slam winners. That said the Munster fly-half can be frustratingly inconsistent. On his day he can produce a kicking masterclass from his siege-gun boot only to follow up with some wayward touchfinders. The Munster fly-half has always been capable of dominating matches, but during the 2009 campaign he showed an impressive range of attacking skills. His sharp handling got Ireland's gifted back-line moving, and he has become arguably the most irreplaceable member of the squad.

Impressive enough against France in the 2009 RBS Six Nations, he kicked flawlessly against the Italians and although he was guilty of some missed tackles, he got off some great offloads. And a yellow card.

O'Gara's flip side was evident against England when he had one of his bad boot days. With better striking he could have put the game to bed on his own. Three missed penalties and a missed conversion are testament enough to a woeful day at the office.

The good Ronan turned up at Murrayfield and the last of his four penalties on the day was a beauty. In the cauldron that was the Millennium Stadium on Championship Saturday it looked like the kicking boots were left at home in Cork in the first half. Fortunately he retrieved them for the second half and his kicking was a big factor in deciding the match; and then, with two minutes of the campaign remaining, with Ireland trailing their hosts by one point, up he stepped for arguably the greatest moment of his international career as he flawlessly and fearlessly drop kicked a Nation to Grand Slam heaven.

After a long apprenticeship, O'Gara is now Europe's Number 1. One of the most improved players in world rugby, the bug eyed American born, Parisian educated, Corkonian, is the living denial of the theory that an old dog cannot learn new tricks. His talents extend far beyond the accuracy of his kicking. His steady advancement towards rugby's defensive traffic has transformed Ireland's options and orchestrated Ireland to their first Grand Slam of the modern era.

O'Gara was born in the American city of San Diego and educated at Presentation Brothers College (PBC), Cork and University College Cork.

His journey to Grand Slam hero is studded with a myriad of record breaking milestones. His career was taking off just when rugby turned professional. He won a Munster Senior Schools Cup medal with PBC in 1995 and followed that two years later with an All-Ireland Under 20 winners' medal with UCC.

In1997 he made his Ireland Under 21 debut against Scotland and that year he joined his present club, Cork Constitution. In 1998 he helped Ireland Under 21s to victory in the Triple Crown and won his first 'A' cap in April 1999, coming on as a replacement against Italy. The following month he was a member of the Cork Constitution side that won the AIB League.

It was his inspirational form for Munster that earned him a senior call-up for the game against England in February 2000. Unfortunately, due to injury, he had to withdraw from the squad but fully fit again, he won his first cap a fortnight later against Scotland at Lansdowne Road, kicking two penalty goals and two conversions. In March 2000 he scored a Six Nations record 30 points against Italy.

During the summer 2000 tour he lost his place to Ulster's David Humphreys, although he did win it back for the autumn Test against Japan, announcing his return with a record-equalling ten conversions.

The battle with Humphreys for the Number 10 jersey was to last until the Ulsterman's retirement in 2006.

O'Gara scored his first international try against Italy in the opening game of the 2000/2001 RBS Six Nations.

He overtook Humphreys as Ireland's record points scorer in the 2006 RBS Six Nations opener against Italy, during which he scored 16 points, including his 8th Test try.

The 2008 Guinness Rugby Writers of Ireland 'Player of the Year' boasts a truly impressive CV including Triple Crown wins in 2004, 2006 and 2007; 13 points in Munster's Heineken Cup final win in 2006 and 11 in the 2008 showdown, both against French opposition and a Magners League title in 2009.

The Six Nations' top points scorer during the 2005, 2006 and 2007 campaigns and the 2009 Championship winning season, he is also the holder of the Heineken Cup's points-scoring record.

O'Gara is Ireland's top points scorer in RBS Six Nations Championship history. He is also Ireland's record points accumulator overall. His 14 dropped goals is another Ireland record and he is currently fifth on the list of world rugby's top points scorers on 919 points.

Memorably, O'Gara was the first points and try scorer for Ireland in their first ever outing at Croke Park in 2007, against France. His half-back partnership with his old school-mate Peter Stringer, although now in its death throes at international level, was world renowned and vital to the causes of Munster and Ireland. The Cork pair made 50 plus Test starts together for Ireland. It has been said that together they could run a game sitting in bathchairs.

He won a first Lions cap, off the bench in the third test against New Zealand in July 2005 having also toured Australia with them in 2001. It was no surprise considering his season that he was named in the Lions squad for the 2009 tour to South Africa.

On a wet and murky November day at Welford Road, O'Gara famously kicked a winning penalty in stoppage time against Leicester from inside his own half, having previously caused some consternation in English rugby circles when he dared suggest that Irish rugby players had no need to be afraid of taking on English opponents. His Munster captain on the day, Paul O'Connell observed:

"If Rog is happy to have a pot, then we're happy to leave him at it. He doesn't like missing, so when he tries a kick you must feel he reckons he can get it."

O'Connell and his comrades, this time in the green of Ireland, backed O'Gara again as the clock ticked down in the Millennium Stadium on 23rd March 2009.

Tomas O'Leary

Born:	**Cork, 22nd October 1983**
Position:	**Scrum Half**
Height:	**1.80m/5'11"**
Weight:	**85 kgs/13st 5lbs**
Province:	**Munster**
Club:	**Dolphin**
Debut for Ireland:	**vs Argentina, May 2007**

Ireland's Cork-born scrum-half Tomas O'Leary confessed prior to the curtain raiser against France in the 2009 RBS Six Nations that he and his teammates were desperate to end their trophy drought.

O'Leary, who was named to make his tournament debut in the game, spoke of his determination to help Ireland end a Championshipless spell stretching back to 1985.

"A lot of the lads here have been chipping away and knocking on the door for the last five or six years aiming to win a Six Nations title," said the Munster Number 9.

"I can definitely see they want to win it badly and I'm no different coming into this environment. I want success. That's all that is going to be acceptable for us. They've been knocking on the door and want it bad.

"The fact we haven't won a Six Nations or even looked like winning a Grand Slam speaks for itself in terms of how difficult a competition it is to win. If we could win a Six Nations it would be a brilliant achievement."

Very prophetic words as the live wire scrum half with the snappy delivery made the Number 9 shirt his own for the duration of the campaign culminating in that elusive and desperately sought after Grand Slam.

O'Leary is now regarded as first choice for both club and country after patiently serving his apprenticeship behind the long-serving Peter Stringer, who, in a reversal of roles, is now the deputy.

O'Leary is grateful to have had such a high-quality mentor, even if it meant he had to bide his time for a regular starting place.

"Peter is a great player," O'Leary said. "I learn what I can from Peter. I still try to do that and the competition is great for both of us. It makes you train harder and develop aspects of your game."

O'Leary rejected suggestions that the Munster and Leinster players place Heineken Cup glory ahead of Six Nations success, adding: 'Definitely not, that's rubbish. "It's the ultimate honour to play for Ireland. You're representing your country."

The Number 9 also welcomed the fact he would be playing alongside Munster teammate and Ireland lynchpin Ronan O'Gara.

"It's great to have that sort of guy beside you for the direction he gives and the experience he has. He is a class footballer as well. He's brilliant to have beside you."

O'Leary honed his skills with Dolphin and the Munster Academy (he was the inaugural winner of the Munster Academy Award for Excellence in 2005). The new boy excelled for Munster in their 2007/08 Heineken Cup-winning campaign, not to mention their Magners League success in 2009.

A son of hurling great Seanie O'Leary, Thomas turned his full focus on rugby after winning an All-Ireland minor medal with Cork. He was part of the Ireland team that reached the 2004 Under 21 World Championship final and has also played for the Irish Sevens side.

He made his full Ireland debut in the 22-20 defeat to Argentina in May 2007.

O'Leary started in every game of the 2009 RBS Six Nations with the exception of the Scotland Test when his mentor took over duties for the day, taking his tally to eight caps against Wales – there will be an awful lot more!

The fact that he has a kicking and running game keeps the opposing back row honest. Against Italy he was shifted to centre after Paddy Wallace's injury, and had less impact. Back on form against England he was as shrewd and enterprising as ever, his clever kicks keeping England on the turn. His excellence on the day meant that although he wouldn't line up at Murrayfield, he was a shoo-in for the crucial finale in Cardiff.

Now a European Champion for club and country, O'Leary was overjoyed at being named in the 2009 Lions squad, but an ankle injury, sustained playing for Munster, ruled him out of the touring party.

ıd

Peter Stringer

Born:	**Cork, 13th December 1977**
Position:	**Scrum-Half**
Height:	**1.70m/5'7"**
Weight:	**72kgs/11st 4lbs**
Province:	**Munster**
Club:	**Shannon**
Debut for Ireland:	**vs Scotland, February 2000**

Some great things come in small packages and the diminutive Munster scrum-half certainly fits that bill. What he lacks in stature and bulk, however, he makes up for in sheer skill and desire and has never been short of feistiness. He possesses a clever whipping pass, an equally clever kick and his tap tackles have become the stuff of legend.

An almost telepathic understanding with his old school mate Ronan O'Gara helped Stringer become an indispensable member of the Ireland squad since his debut against Scotland in February 2000. He has started over 50 Test matches with his old school mate as his half back partner.

A virtual ever-present in the side following his debut, he scored his first international try against Japan in November 2000 and has followed that with efforts against Italy (2003 and 2004), Scotland (2004), the USA (2004) and Wales (2006).

One of the most recognisable players in world rugby, Stringer was a Rugby World Cup Squad member in 2003 and 2007 and has played in three Heineken Cup finals with Munster, collecting winners' medals in 2006 and 2008. He famously left the aggressive, six-footer Biarritz and France flanker Serge Betsen wondering what the hell happened while scoring a solo try that effectively won the game and sealed his Man of the Match performance in the 2006 win over Biarritz. And, in 2009, he was a member of the immortal Grand Slam winning side and added a Magners league title to his collection of honours.

His international success has been a logical progression from his excellent performances for Munster at provincial level. Incredibly, he only missed his first international game due to injury in 2007 when a fractured hand kept him out of the Six Nations match against France.

Educated at Presentation Brothers College Cork and University College Cork, Stringer was a pivotal member of the Irish team for the Triple Crown wins in 2004, 2006 and 2007.

Genuine competition for the Number 9 jersey emerged initially in the shape of Ulster's Isaac Boss and Wasps' Eoin Redden followed by his Munster colleague Tomas O'Leary.

He started the 2007 Rugby World Cup as Ireland's first choice Number 9, only for Eoin Redden to edge past him by the tournament's end. By the time of the 2009 RBS Six Nations he had been reduced to playing second fiddle to O'Leary and managed just one start, against Scotland, but featured in all the other games bar England.

On his first showing in the 2009 RBS Six Nations – against Italy – on initially as a blood replacement for Paddy Wallace, he made an impressive contribution that saw him inspire Ireland to their second try just before half-time; he replaced Thomas O'Leary in the second half and made an impression late on by upping the tempo nicely.

Against Scotland, in his only start, he improved markedly after half-time and some stunning breaks and clever kicking capped a sensational return and had some pundits calling for him to start in the decider in Wales. It was not to be, though, as once again he dropped to the bench in favour of O'Leary. He took over from O'Leary late in the second half as Ireland pressed towards the Holy Grail and Stringer was on hand to inject some much needed urgency.

Although he has lost his grip on the Munster and Ireland Number 9 jerseys, Stringer has battled back and shown that he still has a lot to offer. He is one of an ever expanding band of players closing in on a century of Ireland caps. He won his 89th cap in the decider against Wales and is now fifth in Ireland's all time list as befits a player whose diminutive appearance belies his tenacity and skills.

Stringer has had a stellar provincial and international career and his ultra competitive nature has him wanting more.

Paddy Wallace

Born:	**Belfast, 27th August 1979**
Position:	**Centre/Out-Half**
Height:	**1.8m/5'11"**
Weight:	**81kg/12st 10lbs**
Position:	**Fly Half/Centre**
Club:	**Ballymena**
Province:	**Ulster**
Debut for Ireland:	**vs Pacific Islands, November 2006**

In recent years Paddy Wallace has established himself as Ireland's back-up fly half but he added another string to his bow on the 2008 summer tour when he slotted in superbly well at centre alongside Brian O'Driscoll.

The Belfast man has been with Ulster since 2001 and, owing to David Humphreys' long stranglehold on the number 10 berth, has turned himself into a utility back with the province, capable of playing at 10, 12 or 15.

Far from being a newcomer, the attack-minded and multi-skilled Wallace has been in Ireland senior squads since 2002 but only made his debut as a replacement against South Africa in November 2006.

Along with current senior stalwarts Brian O'Driscoll and Donncha O'Callaghan, he was a member of the Declan Kidney-coached Irish team that won the Under 19 FIRA/World Youth Championship in France in 1998.

He has also represented Ireland at Under 21, 'A', Sevens and senior levels. Some excellent displays for the 'A' team at the 2006 Churchill Cup and for Ulster in the 2006/07 season saw him back in contention for a place in the senior squad.

In undoubtedly one of his best performances in an Irish jersey, he scored 20 points against the All Blacks in an 'A' international at Ravenhill in 2001.

Ireland's strengths in Wallace's chosen positions, however, saw him wait until the 2006 autumn series game against the Pacific Islands for his first full cap. And what a first outing that turned out to be as the 27-year-old's magnificent display comfortably outshone the three full debutants, Jamie Heaslip, Luke Fitzgerald and Stephen Ferris.

In that first Test start he emerged as David Humphreys' natural successor as Ronan O'Gara's understudy by producing a 26-point haul in a near flawless kicking performance against the shell-shocked Islanders. The impressive kicking display was matched by composure in attack, capped with a fully deserved first half try, ensuring Lansdowne Road was given a victorious send off before the bulldozers moved in.

Born in Belfast, he was educated at Mike Gibson's old school, Campbell College, and holds a degree in Business Studies and Marketing from UCD.

He helped his club side, Ballymena, win the AIB League Division One title in 2003, where he played at full-back.

Wallace started in the centre with O'Driscoll for the RBS Six Nations game against France and, although in the blood bin when Ireland's first try was scored, he did enough to maintain his place against Italy, where he was replaced by Gordon D'Arcy having suffered an early injury.

Wallace got the nod for the England game. In justifying the decision Alan Gaffney said that, "Paddy brings different things to the game. He's a very good ball player; he creates space for people on the outside. He's a good reader of the game."

Nevertheless, it was D'Arcy's turn for the Scotland Test and the Wexford man retained the shirt for the decider against Wales with Wallace winning his 16th cap off the bench for Luke Fitzgerald.

Wallace almost became public enemy Number 1 after conceding a late penalty that had Stephen Jones converted, would have shattered Ireland's Grand Slam dream in the cruellest of fashions. Jones missed and a nation and Paddy Wallace could breathe again. Paddy claimed later that he was only "trying to add a bit of drama to the proceedings!" You succeeded.

The Forwards

Rory Best

Born:	**Craigavon, 15th August 1982**
Height:	**1.80m 5'11"**
Weight:	**106kg/16st 7lbs**
Position:	**Hooker**
Club:	**Belfast Harlequins**
Province:	**Ulster**
Debut for Ireland:	**vs New Zealand. November 2005**

A physical front row who packs a punch in the loose, Rory Best became a key member of the Ulster squad during his second full season with the province (2005/2006). His leadership qualities were recognised by Ulster and he was appointed the province's captain for the 2007/08 season. He was also voted Personality of the Year at that season's Ulster Rugby awards.

Educated at Portadown College, Best provides a physical edge up front and solid lineout skills.

The younger brother of former Ireland and Ulster prop Simon, who was forced into retirement due to a heart problem in February 2008, Rory first appeared in a Test as a replacement against New Zealand in 2005. A proficient lineout operator, Best has come a long way since that debut.

He was used off the bench for Marcus Horan in the Wales game for his RBS Six Nations debut in 2006, having graduated through the Ireland Under 21 side at the 2003 World Cup.

It was in that 2006/07 season that his Ireland senior career really took off, taking his chance while others were injured. He played in eight straight matches during that campaign. He muscled his way into the team for the 2006 wins over South Africa and Australia, transferring his provincial form onto the international stage. He scored tries against the Pacific Islanders and against Wales in the 2007 Triple Crown-winning campaign, during which he was ever-present. His power-packed performances saw him become first choice hooker and a cornerstone of the Irish pack.

The powerfully built Best's international career has seen him competing with Shane Byrne and then Jerry Flannery, and sometimes Bernard Jackman for the Number 2 jersey.

The Ulsterman started twice during the 2007 Rugby World Cup and three times in the 2008 RBS Six Nations. He regained the shirt for the June clash with Australia only to be ousted yet again for the 2009 RBS Six Nations by Flannery.

Although Flannery got the nod, Best featured in all five Tests bringing his Test tally to 32. His only start was the Scotland game, replacing Flannery in the other four games.

He replaced Flannery after 48 minutes against France; got 15 minutes to impress against Italy, but the game had cut up by the time he came in and he struggled to make an impression.

Against Scotland he eased concerns about his delivery with a flawless display of darts and he had some supporters calling for a starting berth for the decider in Wales. Again Flannery got the nod, although Best was thrown into the fray as the pressure mounted and helped to see out the game.

Tom Court

Born:	**Brisbane, Australia 6th November 1980**
Height:	**1.91m/6'3"**
Weight:	**122kg/19st 2lbs**
Position:	**Prop**
Province:	**Ulster**
Debut for Ireland:	**vs Italy, February 2009**

A powerfully-built tighthead prop with considerable influence in the loose, Tom Court was the only uncapped player to feature in Ireland's 2009 Six Nations campaign. Court won his first cap as a replacement for Marcus Horan during Ireland's 38-9 victory over Italy. He had been on the bench for the opener against France but was unused. He qualifies to play international rugby for Ireland through his Limerick born grandfather.

Court plies his trade with Ulster as a tighthead and loosehead prop, having primarily played at tighthead in his early career but switched to loosehead in the 2007/2008 season when B. J. Botha arrived to take over at Ulster.

Court began his sporting career as a shot-putter and was Australian University Champion for three years running while attending the University of Queensland. He actually had Olympic trials in 2002.

A late convert to rugby, he disclosed in an interview with the Ulster Rugby Website, that he had begun playing rugby in order to lose weight. His career began in 2004 when he turned out for Manawatu and Queensland Reds before moving to Ulster.

Court actually represented Ireland 'A' at the 2006 Churchill Cup before he had played his first game for Ulster. He was also named in the 2008 Churchill Cup squad and appeared as a substitute in all three games: against USA, England Saxons and a representative Argentina XV. He made his full Ireland debut in an uncapped match against The Barbarians at Kingsholm Stadium in Gloucester in May 2008. A game the New Zealand bound Ireland side won 14-39.

Stephen Ferris

Born:	**Portadown, 2nd August 1985**
Height:	**1.93m/6'4"**
Weight:	**109kg/17st 2lbs**
Position:	**Back Row**
Club:	**Dungannon**
Province:	**Ulster**
Debut for Ireland:	**vs Pacific Islands, November 2006**

It has been said that Superman owns a pair of Stephen Ferris pyjamas. No wonder. One of the outstanding talents of the 2009 RBS Six Nations, Ferris's contribution was immense. He started every match in the Grand Slam winning campaign.

He put in a huge performance against Italy in a match made for a blind-side flanker out to make a name for himself. His carry for Fitzgerald's try was a brave decision followed by a very impressive piece of power and handling and, aside from that, Ferris's sheer strength and determination really stood out all day. That display was followed by a typically robust offering against England. He was always eager and available; splendidly fierce while displaying a range of skills, despite the hours of hard labour he had to put in. Against Scotland at Murrayfield his opening hit set the tone of another day of remorseless aggression from the enforcer. One pundit opined that scientists would have to undertake tests to ascertain whether Ferris's body is composed of granite and steel.

Winning his unlucky 13th cap in the decider against Wales he made a sad departure through injury after just seven minutes, and it was Denis Leamy who quickly picked up the pace of the action and made a major contribution.

A graduate of the Ulster Academy, Ferris won a development contract with the province at the start of the 2005/06 season, and was rewarded with a full contract after impressing Coach Mark McCall.

He played for Ireland at the 2004 IRB Under 19 World Cup and the 2005 IRB Under 21 World Cup, scoring five tries in five appearances at the latter.

Such were his performances during his debut season that Ferris collected the 2005/06 Guinness/Ulster Rugby Young Player of the Year award. He missed out on playing at the 2006 IRB Under 21 World Cup after undergoing an operation to clear up ankle damage but did make his 'A' international that November against Australia A.

He was initially a surprise inclusion in Ireland's squad for the 2006 November Tests, but anyone who watched his rise with Ulster knew exactly what head coach Eddie O'Sullivan saw in him. Combative, strong running and relishing a big hit, he possesses the size, skill and physicality to play anywhere in the back row.

A member of Ireland's 2007 Rugby World Cup squad and 2008 summer tour squad, the Ravenhill favourite is a graduate of the IRFU's High Performance Select Group. His stock had risen so much by the end of the 2009 Six Nations that he was a virtual shoo-in for the 2009 Lions squad.

The Armagh man had to battle back from a series of injuries to continue his fine development with Ulster and Ireland and laid down a marker with a man of the match performance in Ireland's record 55-0 defeat of Canada in November 2008. That performance was shown not to be a flash in the pan by his outstanding contribution to Ireland's Grand Slam success.

Jerry Flannery

Born:	**Galway, 17th October 1978**
Height:	**1.80m/5'11"**
Weight:	**102kg/16st**
Position:	**Hooker**
Club:	**Shannon**
Province:	**Munster**
Debut for Ireland:	**vs Romania, November 2005**

A diamond, albeit a rough diamond, Jerry Flannery has proved himself the true heir of Keith Wood and one of the finds of recent years.

The irrepressible Flannery rose to national prominence on foot of some eye-catching displays for Munster. Strong at the set piece and deceptively quick in the loose, Flannery made the most of an injury to Frankie Sheahan (neck) to impress for the province. His purple patch coincided with a dip in form for Ireland's long-time first choice hooker Shane Byrne that saw Flannery earn a Test call up.

Educated at St. Munchin's College and University College Cork, the publican's son made his Ireland senior debut against Romania in November 2005, coming off the bench as a second-half replacement during the 43-12 victory. His displays for Munster were so impressive that in 2006 he was offered and signed a new three year contract with the province.

Flannery crowned his first start and RBS Six Nations debut against Italy in February 2006 with his first try and he quickly became one of Ireland's first-choice forwards. He was ever-present for the remainder of the 2005/06 season. However, shoulder surgery saw him sidelined for much of 2007.

Rory Best made the hooker berth his own during the 2007 Triple Crown-winning run, relegating Flannery to the bench.

Back fully fit, Flannery fought his way back into contention for the 2008 RBS Six Nations, playing in all five matches but Ulster's Best was the man in possession of the Number 2 jersey for the entire tournament. Thus began a battle royal for the hooker berth which was eventually won by the Munster man with Best being relegated to the role of understudy for the successful 2009 campaign. The only game Flannery didn't start was against Scotland.

A powerful scrummager, he graduated to Test level from his formative days as an Ireland Under 21 player and represented Ireland students while attaining an Economics Degree at the University of Cork.

Originally with Munster, he moved to Connacht but fearful that the squad would not exist the following season, never mind his place in it he made his escape back to Munster.

Flannery has his detractors but he is a warrior of the highest order. Throughout the campaign he produced typically live wire performances and he hit the target with his throwing in some very difficult conditions. He now has 31 Ireland caps, not to mention two AIB League medals, a Celtic Cup medal, two Heineken Cup medals, a Magners League winners' medal, three Triple Crowns and a Grand Slam.

The one blot on Jerry's season came when he had to pull out of the 2009 Lions squad due to an elbow injury that sidelined him for 12 weeks.

John Hayes

Born: Limerick, 2nd November 1973
Height: 1.93m/6'4"
Weight: 125kgs/19st 9lbs
Position: Prop
Club: Bruff R.F.C.
Province: Munster
Debut for Ireland: vs Scotland. February 2000

There weren't many takers for Richard Harris's Bull McCabe's offer to dance in the classic film *The Field*. And not many would accept a similar offer from John "The Bull" Hayes in the battlefields of the Six Nations. Paul O'Connell has described it as an absolute pleasure to play alongside him. And he should know as he plies his trade with him for Munster and Ireland.

At 6'4" and weighing in at almost 20st, John Hayes is one of the biggest front rows in the game. Ireland's relative lack of depth at tighthead has made him the country's most irreplaceable player. Ireland's scrum is widely viewed as one of the team's few weak points with Hayes often bearing the brunt of the criticism. But while the Munster front-row man is not the most destructive scrummager in Test rugby, his contribution in other areas is invaluable. Tremendous upper-body strength has made him a key component in Ireland's line-out success as a lifter, while his lack of mobility is tempered by his work rate at the breakdown.

Hayes has taken the phrase 'durable prop' to another level. Not only was the 2009 RBS Six Nations clash with England his record-breaking 47th successive appearance in the RBS 6 Nations but the cap also brought him level again with Irish caps record holder Malcolm O'Kelly (92). That record is testament to his ability to maintain high levels of fitness and shows how vital the much-loved tighthead is to the Irish cause.

Hayes, the Cappamore farmer and Bruff clubman, of course took it all in his stride, just as he has done ever since he and four other teammates made their Test debuts for Ireland against Scotland back in February 2000.

Speaking about Hayes prior to his record-breaking appearance, Declan Kidney said: "He's just living it, really, rather than working at it.

"I think professionalism in the best sense of the word. I've seen people who get paid who aren't overly professional, and I've seen people who don't get any money for doing something and they're very professional.

"And I think in the best sense of the word that's what John is, in the way that he has managed to look after himself and keep himself as fit as he is.

"And to play in probably the toughest position on the rugby pitch, at tighthead prop, which is the cornerstone of everything you do, certainly in scrummaging.

"His prowess in the lineout is also well seen but to keep the mobility that is needed to go beyond the set pieces, that takes a lot of personal care and professionalism, right down to everything you eat.

"He's not the greatest man for talking about himself but it is his total professionalism really, I don't think that can be over-stated.

"How he goes about it, I don't know. He's quite a private man, and he enjoys that side of it.

"And yet he loves the camaraderie of the team room. I think he would be well noted for the way he looks after himself."

Born in Limerick and educated at Doon CBS[6]. The Bull's achievements in the game are even more incredible when one considers that he only started playing rugby at the late age of 18, when he joined Limerick club side Bruff, lining out as a flanker.

He moved from Bruff to Shannon and after playing two seasons with the Under 20s, helping the club win the All-Ireland League in 1995, moved to New Zealand for two years, playing his rugby with the Marist club in Invercargill.

On his return from New Zealand he rejoined Shannon and played a major role in their AIB All-Ireland League success in 1998, before returning once again to Bruff. It was during his last stint at Shannon and at Invercargill that he metamorphosed from flanker to prop.

That summer he was called into the Ireland Senior squad for the first time for the tour to South Africa.

During the tour he played against Boland, South West Districts, Griqualand West and North West Districts and in November 1998 he played for the Combined Provinces against South Africa in Musgrave Park.

In February 2000, he won his first senior cap against Scotland. He has been a virtual ever-present in the Irish side since, notching up his record 94th cap in the 2009 RBS Six Nations decider against Wales.

He originally came to public attention in starting all ten of Ireland's internationals in the Triple Crown-winning year of 2004. He toured with the Lions to New Zealand in 2005 and proved yet again how vital he is to the Irish cause during the 2006 and 2007 Triple Crown successes. He has continued to amass caps, featuring in every game during the 2007 Rugby World Cup, the 2008 RBS 6 Nations and the Big One: The 2009 Grand Slam. A veritable rock

---

[6] Christian Brothers School

in the Irish scrum and lineout, the teak-tough but softly spoken tighthead still shows no sign of wilting.

He produced strong performances throughout a campaign that also brought personal success as he became the record Ireland caps holder; the record Six Nations appearance record holder and holder of the record for consecutive Six Nations appearances. He helped Munster to Magners league success in 2009 but the Grand Slam is the crowning glory of a wonderful career. He was a late call up to the 2009 Lions squad following an injury to Euan Murray.

Last word on Hayes goes to a novice 10 years his junior, Jamie Heaslip: "You can't say enough about the man. He just makes my life so easy to attack it is a joke! At 50 years old and he is still pulling these games out of the hat!"

(

Jamie Heaslip

Born:	**Tiberias, Israel 15th December 1983**
Height:	**1.93m/6'4"**
Weight:	**109kg/17st 1lb**
Position:	**No. 8**
Club:	**Naas**
Province:	**Leinster**
Debut for Ireland:	**vs Pacific Islands, November 2006**

Jamie Heaslip has a bright future in an area of fierce competition within Ireland's squad – the back row. The Leinster Number 8 has wonderful skills, but is also an imposing physical presence around the pitch.

A well-balanced runner, he had been knocking at Ireland's door for a while and it opened as Eddie O'Sullivan named him in his 22 for the opening RBS Six Nations clash against Italy in 2008. He made the Ireland Number 8 jersey his own during that campaign and kept it for the 2009 campaign, starting all but one of the five tests. Denis Leamy took over for the Scotland game while Heaslip took Leamy's place on the bench.

He produced two excellent displays in the opening games of the 2009 RBS Six Nations. An outstanding try against the French in the curtain raiser was almost replicated in Rome, only to be thwarted by a last-ditch tackle a metre or so short of the Italian line. He produced a strong display in which he showed plenty of the superior speed and footwork that separates him from Denis Leamy.

By the time England arrived in the capital the secret was out and they were looking for him. Nevertheless, he was consistent in all aspects. Against Scotland, he scored the only try of the contest to set Ireland up for their tilt at the Grand Slam.

A son of former Shannon player Richard Heaslip, a Colonel in the Irish Army, the Leinster back rower progressed steadily up through the ranks. After starring for Dublin University and the Ireland Under 21s, (whom he helped finish second at the 2004 Under 21 World Cup, losing in the final to New Zealand, while earning himself an IRB Under 21 Player of the Year nomination) he made his Leinster senior debut in the Celtic League in March 2005.

He took his Ireland 'A' caps haul to six in the November 2006 game with Australia and was widely recognised as Ireland's best player at the 2006 Churchill Cup.

Heaslip has the honour of being the 1000th player to wear the green of Ireland, making his debut against the Pacific Islanders in November 2006. He failed to make the 2007 Rugby World Cup squad but bounced back to start Ireland's last six Test matches, prior to the Guinness series 2008.

Heaslip, who started playing rugby with local club Naas, has a degree in Medical Mechanical Engineering. He has lined out for Dublin University and Clontarf but has gone back to his roots with Naas.

One of the major successes of the 2009 tournament, Heaslip, as well as winning his 18th cap against Wales, collected the first international honours of his career in winning the Triple Crown and the Grand Slam. Further honours followed in the form of a Lions call up for the 2009 tour and a try scoring performance in Leinster's maiden Heineken Cup success over Leicester also in 2009.

Marcus Horan

Born:	Limerick, 7th September 1977
Height:	1.85m/6'1"
Weight:	105 kgs/16st 7lbs
Position:	Prop
Club:	Shannon
Province:	Munster
Debut for Ireland:	vs USA, June 2000

A dynamic ball carrier with a turn of pace that belies his position as a prop, Marcus Horan has bedded into the Ireland team as first-choice loosehead in recent years and is now a crucial part of the set up. Having played a supporting role to Peter Clohessy and Reggie Corrigan for years, the Munster man has carved out an impressive international career for himself.

Twice an All-Ireland title winner with Shannon, he was initially used by Ireland as an impact player off the bench. He played second fiddle to Leinster veteran Corrigan for the 2003 World Cup (although he actually appeared in all five games in the competition) and in the 2004 and 2005 RBS Six Nations campaigns.

Horan's fine performances for both province (he was outstanding during Munster's Heineken Cup-winning run in 2006) and country catapulted him back into the Ireland starting line-up. And he cemented his place as Ireland's first choice number one in 2005-2006 playing in all four Six Nations victories as well as starting all three summer Tests as his rival neared the end of his Test career.

He was ever-present during the 2007 Rugby World Cup and missed just one game of that year's Six Nations due to injury. He scored his sixth Test try in spectacular fashion against Scotland in the 2008 Six Nations, when he was once again ever-present. That same year he collected another Heineken Cup winners' medal as Munster triumphed in Europe for the second time in two seasons.

An Ireland Under 21 international, he won his first 'A' cap against England in February 2000 and was a regular in the side for all of that season. In May 2000, he was called into the senior squad and came on as a replacement in the non-cap game against the Barbarians. He then went on the summer tour of the Americas and won his first senior cap as a replacement for Paul Wallace against the US Eagles in June 2000. In November of that year Marcus scored a try for Ireland Under 25s in their defeat of Japan.

Having won eight 'A' caps, all as a replacement, he won his second full cap, over two years after his debut, against Fiji in November 2002 and recorded his first senior try in the 64-7 destruction of Namibia in Sydney in the 2003 World Cup.

Educated at St. Munchin's College and the Limerick Institute of Technology, Horan, an honest scrummager who is as comfortable at home as he is in the trenches, played in every game in the 2009 Six Nations, taking his caps tally to 66.

He put in a typically marauding display in the loose against France, before being replaced by Tom Court due to injury in the 54th minute. Against Italy, he had a tough afternoon in parts with the obdurate Castrogiovanni opposite, although he wasn't too flustered and dealt with it well enough, and also carried nicely when he got on the ball.

As expected he did his job solidly in the tight and loose exchanges throughout the campaign. And, although not as prominent in the games against the Triple Crown Nations, he is the type of player who can always be guaranteed to give it everything. His patience in the early days of his international career was rewarded with a well deserved Grand Slam Winners' medal.

A Magners league winner's medal with Munster capped a very productive season for Horan.

Denis Leamy

Born:	**Tipperary, 27th November 1981**
Position:	**Back Row (No 8)**
Height:	**1.88m /6'2"**
Weight:	**108kg/17st**
Club:	**Cork Constitution**
Province:	**Munster**
Debut for Ireland:	**vs USA, November 2004**

"Definitely we want to go out and prove to everyone that we can put big games together in successive weeks and show people exactly what we have to offer, to put ourselves up there among the top teams in the world."

Such is the esteem in which Denis Leamy is held among the Irish rugby faithful that one fan posted the following tribute to Leamy on the Bebo website: "The popular videogame 'Doom' is based loosely around the time Satan borrowed two bucks from Denis Leamy and forgot to pay him back. Leamy sold his soul to the devil for his ability to never feel pain and unparalleled strength. Shortly after the transaction was finalised, Leamy bounced the devil before dumping him on his ass and taking his soul back. The devil, who appreciates irony, couldn't stay mad and admitted he should have seen it coming. They now play poker every second Wednesday of the month."

In 2006 Leamy was announced as the rugby winner in Ireland's national sports star awards. With Brian O'Driscoll and Paul O'Connell still alive and kicking, it is not easy to claim any prize in Irish rugby. The poacher fiend is approaching his illustrious colleagues in terms of world stature.

A relentless ball-carrier, who also relishes his defensive duties, his stock in Test rugby has risen remarkably since making his debut against the USA in 2004. Since that time, the versatile Leamy has broadened Ireland's back row options. In his first six

Test appearances, he lined out both as an openside flanker and at Number 8, taking over from his provincial colleague, Anthony Foley at the base of the Irish scrum for the 2005 autumn internationals.

The Tipperary hurling fan was raised on the family's beef farm at Dualla a few miles from Cashel. He was educated at Rockwell College, with whom he won a Munster Junior Cup, and University College Cork.

His development continued as an Ireland Schools and Under 21 international. On-pitch indiscipline, long since eradicated, cost him a place on Ireland's 2002 Under 21 World Cup squad.

And while a knee injury curtailed his involvement with Munster in 2003/04, he returned the following season with his performances earning him his first Ireland call-up.

Leamy made his Six Nations debut against Italy in 2005, but missed the remaining games of that championship due to a hamstring injury.

Ireland and Leamy took a Triple Crown from the 2006 Six Nations with his highlight being a try against England at Twickenham. Reputations were also enhanced from rematches with New Zealand and Australia that summer. Having been soundly trounced by the Southern Hemisphere giants the previous autumn, Ireland turned in vastly improved performances. A typically blockbusting display in the New Zealand game drew rich praise from the All Blacks management. This was followed by Leamy's demolition work against South Africa when Ireland defeated the Springboks by 32-15 at Lansdowne Road.

Another Triple Crown was added in 2007 and, as in 2006, Leamy played in every game. He also featured in every game of the 2009 Grand Slam Campaign, getting his only start against Scotland.

He replaced Jamie Heaslip on 68 minutes against England, closing out the game with a typically robust tackle on Tom Croft. He replaced the unfortunate Stephen Ferris after only eight minutes in the final game against Wales, winning his 39th cap.

A player who possesses a quite rapturous style of play that features shovel-like foraging hands, run-all-day energy and explosive strength, Leamy won the Heineken Cup with Munster in 2006, scoring his side's only try in the final, and again in 2008. He also added a Magners League winners' medal in 2009.

Donncha O'Callaghan

Born:	**Cork, 24th March 1979**
Height:	**1.98m /6'6"**
Weight:	**110kgs /17st 4lbs**
Position:	**Lock/Second Row**
Club:	**Cork Constitution**
Province:	**Munster**
Debut for Ireland:	**v Wales, March 2003**

The last decade or so must seem like a whirlwind to Ireland's rugged second row, Donncha O'Callaghan. He won international recognition for the first time, lining up against England Schools in Lansdowne Road in March 1997; in 1998 he was a member of the Declan Kidney coached Ireland team that won the FIRA Under 19 World Youth championship; Under 21 honours followed less than a year later when he made his debut as a replacement for Bob Casey in the game against Wales.

In November 2000 he represented Ireland at Under 25 level (vs Japan) and in November 2001 played for the Ireland Development vs Samoa in Donnybrook. The inevitable first 'A' cap arrived when he came on as a replacement against Scotland at Ravenhill (March 2002) and a year later he won his first senior cap as a replacement against Wales in Cardiff in 2003. He added two further caps later that year and won seven more off the bench before winning his place in the starting XV for the RBS Six Nations game against Wales in February 2004, his first full start.

If that wasn't enough, he played in the Rugby World Cup in 2003 and again in 2007 and played his part in Ireland's three Triple Crown triumphs and Grand Slam, not to mention his part in Munster's Heineken Cup success in 2006 and 2008 and their Magners League triumph in 2009.

O'Callaghan prospered during the Lions' tour of New Zealand in the summer of 2005, where he started the final two Tests and returned home with an enhanced reputation.

There is no more ferocious battleground for positions than Ireland's second row, where the lively, rumbustious, no-nonsense O'Callaghan and Malcolm O'Kelly duel for the right to partner Paul O'Connell.

O'Callaghan, who was on bench duty for much of his early international career, gradually blossomed – being ever-present for the last four Six Nations championships and helping to cement his Munster second row partnership with Paul O'Connell at Test level.

He led the race during the autumn of 2008, when he was picked against South Africa and Australia, with O'Kelly having to settle for a start against the Pacific Islanders, but the initiative has now swung irreversibly in the Munster giant's direction.

Educated at Christian Brothers College, Cork, by the time of the start of the 2009 RBS Six Nations O'Callaghan was O'Connell's undisputed partner. He had come an awful long way since his junior days at Highfield RFC.

The ever-faithful foil to O'Connell in the engine-room, O'Callaghan is a genuine grafter who always puts his body on the line. His worth to Ireland was evident as he played every minute of every game in the Championship taking his caps tally to 55. His first and only try for Ireland to date came against France in 2006.

In the opening games against France and Italy he was tenacious in the tackle; exuding dynamism on the front foot and was very effective at securing the ball at the breakdown. O'Callaghan got stuck in against a fired-up Italian Number 8 that contested every ruck.

He kept up his high standards in the three remaining games, always playing his part in Ireland's success at the lineout, and making crucial contributions in the tight.

If Donncha O'Callaghan's second-row partner didn't exist, forests of newsprint would be dedicated to this man's worth during the Six Nations; suffice to say, as supporting roles go, O'Callaghan's is meatier than most. Few deserved this Grand Slam, and the Lions call-up that followed, more.

Paul O'Connell

Born:	**Limerick, 20th October 1979**
Height:	**1.98m/6'6"**
Weight:	**111kgs/17st 7lbs**
Position:	**Lock**
Club:	**Young Munster**
Province:	**Munster**
Debut for Ireland:	**vs Wales, February 2002**

"A perfectly hewn lump of Limerick granite. A warrior and an athlete. The Lion King in waiting."

Large, fiery in hair and in temperament, stroppy and influential, Paul O'Connell is the engine that drives Ireland. Another of Ireland's world class performers, he is regarded by many as the most inspirational forward in Europe and probably the best second row in the world. He would make a World XV in the second row and deserves to be ranked above legends like Slattery, Duggan, and fellow second row Lenihan.

His presence recalls the prime of Martin Johnson for England and Leicester. And in the pale blue eyes, two pools of ice beneath that fiery red hair, is the same withering disregard for slackers patented by that other local legend Roy Keane. His Ireland and Munster teammates concede they would only be half as potent without him. 'We call him Keano or Roy because that's the kind of influence he is in our squad," confirms his second row partner Donncha O'Callaghan.

"He sets the standard and if you don't perform, even in training, he'll let you know. Paulie's a bit of a colossus. You know that if you put your body on the line for the bollox he'll do the same for you. If Paul makes a big tackle I'll want to do the same. He's a huge man in that way. He'll set a tone. It's as if he's the heartbeat of our pack."

Stories about his scary commitment are relatively common place but his former captain at Munster, Anthony Foley insists the public don't know the half of it: "At times I've had to ask Paulie to tone it down in training – not so much for his own sake but for the sake of the other fellas around him – they just can't do what he can."

Limerick through and through, the youngest of three boys he was born in Drombana, a townland on the outskirts of the city and received his early schooling at Ard Scoil Ris in Limerick. He followed his dad, Mick, into the Young Munster club and studied computer science at the local university

At the age of 10, he dedicated himself to swimming; five mornings and evenings a week. His dedication paid off and he became a national junior champion. He only gave up when he sensed he was not quick enough to make the 1996 Olympics. He took up golf and was down to a three handicap within two years and still plays off single figures. In rugby he combines this natural athleticism with a murderous intensity. As the former Ireland captain and fellow Munster man, Keith Wood, once put it: "things happen when Paul joins a ruck or maul."

The callow O'Connell played on the same Ireland Schools side as Gordon D'Arcy and the early seeds of his second row partnership with Donncha O'Callaghan were sown when he played in five consecutive games for the Irish Under 21s with him as his second row partner.

He won his first full cap in February 2002 against Wales and marked the occasion by scoring his first international try in what was Eddie O'Sullivan's first game in charge.

O'Connell has been virtually ever-present since then, taking his caps tally to 62 with six tries, including the last ever Test try at the old Lansdowne Road, against the Pacific Islanders in November 2007.

Ireland captain in the absence of Brain O'Driscoll, O'Connell has led his country on four occasions and famously skippered Munster to Heineken Cup glory in 2008 and to Magners League success a year later.

Short listed for the 2006 IRB player of the year award, the only northern hemisphere player among the five nominees, he was voted the Guinness Rugby Writers' Player of the Year in 2006, and, during the 2005/06 campaign, was also named as the IRUPA[7] Player of the Year, the Munster Rugby Supporters Club Player of the Year and the Irish Rugby Supporters Club Player of the Year.

Hard, uncompromising, mobile, an excellent lineout jumper, and destructive ball carrier with the speed of a back row forward on those long legs – the Munster lock is the complete package and a galvanising force in the Irish pack. He brought all of those attributes to the 2009 RBS Six Nations.

Player of the tournament for many observers in the 2009 RBS Six Nations; against France he was key in the forwards and dominated the lineouts Colossus-style, and was an inspiration throughout. The skipper in all but name. Against Italy he was majestic in the air and a powerful carrier and workhorse on the deck. Ireland needed physical leadership and O'Connell supplied it in spades.

In the dire spectacle that was the England Test he was once again superb and yet again was almost unchallenged at the lineout, an absolutely magnificent warrior in phase after phase. He was not just meeting expectations, he was exceeding them.

The awe-inspiring momentum was maintained at Murrayfield where he produced another astonishing performance of raw, brutish physicality with the intelligence to know where to be and where to carry at all times during the game. He took on a vast amount of ball and was imperious in the air.

---

[7] Irish Rugby Union Players' Association

A towering performance against Wales confirmed not only Ireland as Grand Slam Champions but Paul O'Connell as the captain of the Lions for the 2009 tour of South Africa when he will be keen to make up for the disappointment of the 2005 Lions' tour.

No one deserved these accolades more.

Mick O'Driscoll

Born:	**Cork, 8th October 1978**
Height:	**1.96cm/6'5"**
Weight:	**108kg/17st**
Position:	**Lock**
Province:	**Munster**
Club:	**Cork Constitution**
Debut for Ireland:	**vs Romania, June 2001**

Is this the man with the toughest job in rugby, trying to dislodge the triumvirate of Malcolm O'Kelly, Paul O'Connell and Donnacha O'Callaghan?

Since making his debut in a 37-3 victory over Romania in Bucharest in June 2001, Mick O'Driscoll has managed to accumulate just 17 caps, 12 of which have been won as a replacement, giving some indication of the enormity of the task facing him.

A former class mate of Peter Stringer at Presentation Brothers College, Cork, he won a schools' rugby medal in 1996. He also played GAA[8] at underage level with Éire Óg in Cork.

O'Driscoll, who came up through the Munster ranks, schools and under 21s, made his debut for the province in 1998 against Neath. He went on to represent Munster regularly in both the Celtic League and the European Cup, before a move to French side Perpignan at the end of the 2002/2003 season.

The former UCC and Cork Constitution second row had clearly impressed Perpignan with his performances against them in the pool stages of the Heineken Cup that season.

---

[8] Gaelic Athletic Association

He returned to Munster in 2005, having played regularly in the French side's back row and has since become an important member of the squad.

He was on the replacements bench for Munster's 2006 Heineken Cup win and replaced captain Anthony Foley for the last 10 minutes of the 2008 victorious showdown against Toulouse. He added a Magners League winners' medal to his collection in 2009.

A former Ireland 'A' captain, the towering Corkman captained Munster against the All Blacks in November 2008 for the 30th anniversary of that legendary 12-0 win over the tourists at Thomond Park in 1978.

O'Driscoll beat off the challenge of Leinster's Leo Cullen to secure his place in the squad for the 2006 Six Nations. He added two more caps in 2007 Six Nations and featured in all games in 2008

Such was the stranglehold his Munster colleagues, O'Callaghan and O'Connell, had on the second row positions O'Driscoll never got off the replacements bench in the 2009 campaign, having been last capped against England at Twickenham in the final game of the 2008 campaign.

Malcolm O'Kelly

Born:	**Chelmsford, 19th July 1974**
Height:	**2.03cm/6'8"**
Weight:	**117kgs/18st 5lbs**
Position:	**Lock**
Province:	**Leinster**
Club:	**St Mary's College**
Debut for Ireland:	**vs New Zealand, November 1997**

Ireland's Essex born "Malcolm in the Middle" with a Masters in Maths, became Ireland's most capped player when he lined up against Scotland in 2005, for his 70th cap, exceeding the 69 the legendary centre Mike Gibson won from 1964-79. O'Kelly celebrated the occasion with his seventh international try.

His performance on his Ireland debut against New Zealand in 1997 helped him gain a foothold in the side and he was then ever-present for 12 consecutive internationals and has been featuring in Irish sides every year since, only missing out due to injuries.

Malcolm O'Kelly was educated at Templeogue College and Trinity College, where he gained his Masters Degree.

During the 1994/95 season he made his Ireland Under 21 debut against Wales and made his Leinster Senior debut against Northern Transvaal.

In the summer of 1996 he played for Ireland Students in the World Cup in South Africa, and toured with the Development squad to New Zealand and Western Samoa the following year.

O'Kelly was a member of the Lions squad for the summer 2001 tour. He missed the 2005 Lions tour to New Zealand because of a groin problem, having played in 23 of Ireland's 24 games up to the end of the 2005 RBS Six Nations.

He played at both the 1999 and 2003 Rugby World Cups and was a Triple Crown winner in 2004, 2006 and 2007 and a Heineken Cup winner in 2009.

Despite a laid back appearance, O'Kelly is an accomplished lineout operator whose mobility makes him conspicuous in the loose. His Test haul of eight tries includes efforts against Scotland (2), Argentina, the USA, Russia, Wales, Italy and the Pacific Islanders, whom he scored against in the last ever international at the old Lansdowne Road stadium in November 2007.

O'Kelly looks to have succumbed to Donncha O'Callaghan in the battle to partner Paul O'Connell in Ireland's second row. He began the 2009 tournament as Ireland's most capped player on 91 caps and took his tally to 92 when he replaced Paul O'Connell at the fag end of the Italy game. He finished the tournament in joint third place on the caps table with Ronan O'Gara, having been overtaken by John Hayes and Brian O'Driscoll.

Alan Quinlan

Born:	**Tipperary, 13th July 1974**
Position:	**Back Row**
Height:	**1.91m/6'3"**
Weight:	**105 kgs/16st 7lbs**
Province:	**Munster**
Club:	**Shannon**
Debut for Ireland:	**v Romania, October 1999**

Alan Quinlan was in reflective mood in the aftermath of winning his 26th cap in the 55-0 stroll in the park against Canada in November 2008. Veteran flanker Quinlan admitted that he feels like the 'old man' of Declan Kidney's youthful Ireland squad, but claimed he has been rejuvenated by the arrival of his former provincial boss on the international scene.

The 34-year-old came off the bench to score the penultimate and best of his country's six tries in the slaughter of Canada at Thomond Park.

The combative and workman-like back rower Quinlan bravely fought his way back into the Ireland squad after suffering a number of injury blows. He dislocated his shoulder at the 2003 World Cup, while scoring the crucial try in the vital pool win over Argentina that booked Ireland's place in the quarter finals. He scored a total of three tries at that World Cup before his untimely injury, the other two coming against Namibia.

A cruciate ligament injury to his right knee meant the 2005/06 season was almost a complete write-off, but the Tipperary man worked his way back to full fitness and, in May 2006, won both the AIB League Division One title with Shannon and the Heineken Cup with Munster.

Regarded as one of the hardest opponents in a forwards battle, he came back into the international reckoning with a start against

Argentina in June 2007 and though he was selected in the 2007 Rugby World Cup squad, he failed to make the match day squads.

Educated at Abbey CBS in Tipperary, and a product of Clanwilliam RFC, Quinlan earned representative honours with the Ireland Youths and 'A' team – he was a regular for the latter between 1998 and 2001. He made his senior debut at the 1999 World Cup as a replacement against Romania, and made his Six Nations bow against Italy in 2001.

Now 35, this streetwise campaigner may be in the autumn of his career but he still has an awful lot to offer both province and country. Although named in the 2009 Six Nations squads, he failed to make the final 22 for the five Tests. Nevertheless, the popular Quinlan insisted he is just happy to be involved in an international set-up refreshed by the arrival of Kidney.

"It's an exciting place to be at the moment with all the new coaches and people involved, there's a bit of momentum building and we'll all keep our feet on the ground.

"No matter what age you are it's exciting to be involved in it," he said. "There's renewed enthusiasm. We're all happy going to training. Everybody's working really hard and it's good to be involved in something like that. But we know we'll be judged on performances so we won't get carried away. Hopefully I can stay involved. Declan and the coaches have said that, if you put on an Ireland jersey, you treasure it. And that's the attitude that's coming out in training. It's a good place to be at the moment and hopefully I can stay in the squad."

Having failed to feature for Ireland during the successful RBS Six Nations campaign, Quinlan thought his chance of making this summer's Lions tour was gone. But, thanks to his undeniable form in the Test-like setting of the Heineken Cup, he forced his way into the Lions management's thinking and secured a well-deserved place on the tour plane to South Africa.

His joy was short lived however as he was cited for making eye contact with Leinster's Leo Cullen in the Heineken Cup semi-final; an aberration that cost him a 12-week ban and his seat on the plane to South Africa.

David Wallace

Born:	Limerick, 8th July 1976
Height:	1.88m/6'2"
Weight:	103kg/16st 2lbs
Position:	Back Row
Club:	Garryowen
Province:	Munster
Debut for Ireland:	vs Argentina, June 2000

Similar to a Matrioshka, (that's a Russian Nesting Doll), if you were to break David Wallace open you would find another David Wallace inside, only smaller and angrier.

The Crescent College Comprehensive and RTC[9] Cork-educated flanker first toured with the Ireland Development Squad in 1997 before winning caps at Under 21 and 'A' level.

He won his first Ireland cap against Argentina in 2000, and was in and out of the team before being ever-present for the 2002 RBS Six Nations. He then found himself in and out of the Irish squad due to three long-term injuries, playing only seven times between the summers of 2003 and 2005.

Keith Gleeson's injury in the 2004 RBS Six Nations opened the door once again for Wallace, "I was having a bit of a schools' reunion with mates from Crescent College; we had won the cup 10 years previously and were watching the Italian game and saw Keith get injured. They all started looking at me saying, 'are you going to stop drinking now'?"

He scored Ireland's most decisive try in the 2004 Triple Crown winning season, then contracted chicken pox a few weeks later which ruled him out of Munster's Heineken Cup semi-final defeat to Wasps the following weekend.

---

[9] Regional Technical College Cork

He was a mid-tour call-up for the 2001 Lions, and again a mid-tour call-up in New Zealand with Ireland the following summer and he was also asked to drop everything and join Eddie O'Sullivan mid-World Cup in Australia in 2003.

Having travelled to South Africa in the summer of 2004 as his country's first choice open side, his priority became to force himself back into Munster reckoning after a season of injury and illness.

Helped by his high quality run-outs in Munster's two Heineken Cup-winning seasons in 2006 and 2008 and their Magners league success in 2009, he has had a strong grip on the Ireland Number 7 jersey ever since.

Johnny O'Connor's foraging work, support play and speed to the breakdown were sacrificed for the threat offered by Wallace in attack, especially as an explosive runner and ball carrier. His speed and power enable him to punch holes in opposition defences, and his defence is solid.

Now, the rugged flanker is an essential part of any Ireland squad – he was ever-present for the 2007 Rugby World Cup and the 2008 Six Nations.

Furthermore he has become central to the Irish lineout where he was often at the tail end in previous years. His talents have drawn him more specifically into Ireland's plans and set pieces. He played in every minute of every game in the 2009 Grand Slam campaign, synchronising his caps and points tally (55 of each) by scoring a superb 11th international try in the defeat of Italy. Wallace had a fantastic campaign: always where the action is at its fiercest; absolutely first class, a man running on everlasting batteries and incapable of taking a backward step. Yet another Irish shoo-in for the 2009 Lions tour.

His brothers Paul and Richard are both former Ireland internationals and Lions tourists. David, however, is the first in the family to amass 50 caps.

The Matches

2009 RBS Six Nations Fixture Schedule

Saturday 7th February 2009

England vs Italy (Twickenham) 3:00pm

Ireland vs France (Croke Park) 5:00pm

Sunday 8th February 2009

Scotland vs Wales (Murrayfield) 3:00pm

Saturday 14th February 2009

France vs Scotland (Stade de France) 3:00pm

Wales vs England (Millennium Stadium) 5:30pm

Sunday 15th February 2009

Italy vs Ireland (Stadio Flaminio) 2:30pm

Friday 27th February 2009

France vs Wales (Stade de France) 8:00pm

Saturday 28th February 2009

Scotland vs Italy (Murrayfield) 3:00pm

Ireland vs England (Croke Park) 5:30pm

Saturday 14th March 2009

Italy vs Wales (Stadio Flaminio) 3:00pm

Scotland vs Ireland (Murrayfield) 5:00pm

Sunday 15th March 2009

England vs France (Twickenham) 3:00pm

Saturday 21st March 2009

Italy vs France (Stadio Flaminio) 1:15pm

England vs Scotland (Twickenham) 3:30pm

Wales vs Ireland (Millennium Stadium) 5:30pm

The bookies installed reigning Grand Slam Champions Wales as 2/1 favourites, who could disagree? France was quoted at 3/1 second favourites, which seemed fair enough, with Ireland a reasonable 7/2 and England at 4/1. Then the odds lengthened with Scotland quoted at 16/1 and Italy 100/1 outsiders.

Round 1
Saturday 7th February 2009
Ireland vs France

Ireland coach Declan Kidney announced a reduced 27-man squad for the opening game against France. This panel remained constant for the duration of the tournament. Only 22 of the 27 actually got time on the pitch.

Fourteen forwards were included in the panel, with Ulster's uncapped prop Tom Court retained with the senior squad.

The other members of the initial RBS Six Nations Squad moved into a 22-man Ireland 'A' squad.

IRELAND SQUAD (vs France, 2009 RBS Six Nations Championship, Croke Park, Saturday, February 7th, kick-off 5.00pm):

Backs:

Tommy Bowe (Ospreys)

Girvan Dempsey (Terenure College – Leinster)

Gordon D'Arcy (Lansdowne – Leinster)

Keith Earls (Young Munster – Munster)

Luke Fitzgerald (Blackrock College – Leinster)

Shane Horgan (Boyne – Leinster)

Robert Kearney (UCD – Leinster)

Geordan Murphy (Leicester)

Brian O'Driscoll (UCD – Leinster) (capt)

Ronan O'Gara (Cork Constitution – Munster)

Tomas O'Leary (Dolphin —Munster)

Peter Stringer (Shannon – Munster)

Paddy Wallace (Ballymena – Ulster)

Forwards:

Rory Best (Banbridge – Ulster)

Tom Court (Malone – Ulster)*

Stephen Ferris (Dungannon – Ulster)

Jerry Flannery (Shannon – Munster)

John Hayes (Bruff – Munster)

Jamie Heaslip (Naas – Leinster)

Marcus Horan (Shannon – Munster)

Denis Leamy (Cork Constitution – Munster)

Donncha O'Callaghan (Cork Constitution – Munster)

Paul O'Connell (Young Munster – Munster)

Mick O'Driscoll (Cork Constitution – Munster)

Malcolm O'Kelly (St. Mary's College – Leinster)

Alan Quinlan (Shannon – Munster)

David Wallace (Garryowen – Munster)

(* Uncapped player)

In Declan Kidney's first Ireland team for the RBS Six Nations Brian O'Driscoll and Paddy Wallace, who had started together in the midfield during the 2008 summer tour to New Zealand and Australia, were paired again for the first time at home.

Robert Kearney was selected at full-back with his Leinster colleague, Luke Fitzgerald named on the left wing, with Tommy Bowe making up the back-three.

Ronan O'Gara and Tomas O'Leary were called upon to continue their provincial partnership at out-half and scrum half respectively.

Among the forwards, Jerry Flannery was chosen at hooker. Also named in the front row were Marcus Horan and John Hayes, who was set for his 90th cap and his 45th consecutive appearance in the Six Nations.

Donncha O'Callaghan and Paul O'Connell were named in the second row together for the 23rd time at international level.

The back row trio of Stephen Ferris, David Wallace and Jamie Heaslip remained in place from the side that started against Argentina in November 2008.

Ulster's Tom Court, the only uncapped player in the Ireland panel, was called upon to provide prop cover on the replacements bench.

IRELAND TEAM & REPLACEMENTS (vs France, 2009 RBS Six Nations Championship, Croke Park, Saturday, February 7th, kick-off 5.00pm):

15 - Robert Kearney (UCD – Leinster)

14 - Tommy Bowe (Ospreys)

13 - Brian O'Driscoll (UCD – Leinster) (capt)

12 - Paddy Wallace (Ballymena – Ulster)

11 - Luke Fitzgerald (Blackrock College – Leinster)

10 - Ronan O'Gara (Cork Constitution – Munster)

9 - Tomas O'Leary (Dolphin – Munster)

1 - Marcus Horan (Shannon – Munster)

2 - Jerry Flannery (Shannon – Munster)

3 - John Hayes (Bruff – Munster)

4 - Donncha O'Callaghan (Cork Constitution – Munster)

5 - Paul O'Connell (Young Munster – Munster)

6 - Stephen Ferris (Dungannon – Ulster)

7 - David Wallace (Garryowen – Munster)

8 - Jamie Heaslip (Naas – Leinster)

Replacements:

16 - Rory Best (Banbridge – Ulster)

17 - Tom Court (Malone – Ulster)

18 - Malcolm O'Kelly (St. Mary's College – Leinster)

19 - Denis Leamy (Cork Constitution – Munster)

20 - Peter Stringer (Shannon – Munster)

21 - Gordon D'Arcy (Lansdowne – Leinster)

22 - Geordan Murphy (Leicester)

Not considered due to injury:

Keith Earls (Young Munster - Munster)

Ireland (13) 30

Tries: Heaslip, O'Driscoll, D'Arcy Cons: O'Gara 3 Pens: O'Gara 3

France (10) 21

Tries: Harinordoquy, Medard Con: Beauxis Drop-goals: Beauxis 2 Pen: Beauxis

Despite having failed to put the French to the sword since 2001, losing six successive games to them in the meantime, an air of optimism pervaded a Croke Park bursting at the seams with anticipation... could the fizzle of Munster be injected by the new management team into an Ireland side that no further away than the autumn internationals looked tired and jaded. Could the Golden Generation at last deliver to a Nation expectant for nigh on five years? Would O'Gara, O'Connell and O'Driscoll et al. finally, finally live up to the hype and finally guillotine the nemesis to set up a platform for a real charge at the Holy Grail: that elusive first Grand Slam of the modern era?

From the early stages the French plan was obvious. They were determined to run at the opposition defence and the Irish were rescued in the seventh minute when Thierry Dusautoir knocked on just short of the line. More French attacks followed but desperate Irish defence and a couple of impressive catches by Rob Kearney kept the visitors at bay.

The French coach had promised that his team would run and handle. He wasn't bluffing. In a wonderfully sweeping move on 14 minutes which began from deep with Florian Fritz ploughing through O'Gara's tackle and gathering momentum from Maxime Medard's grubber along the right touchline for Fulgence Ouedraogo. From the ruck, France moved the ball wide and a long cut out pass found Sebastian Chabal in space and Julian Malzieu sent the recalled Harinordoquy over with an inside pass that looked marginally forward. Beauxis added the conversion to give the visitors a 7-3 lead and wiping out Ronan O'Gara's early penalty.

France spoiled a glorious try by going off their feet at the restart allowing O'Gara to kick Ireland a mere point behind their increasingly dominant visitors. Ireland was at this stage living off scraps.

A tight forward drive into French territory yielded a chance for the hosts to get their noses in front in the 31st minute but O'Gara fluffed his lines from 45 metres, setting Irish nerves jangling as only he can. The disappointment of that miss was short lived as three minutes later Croke Park erupted in wild delight as Ireland forged ahead after conjuring up one of their best passages of play of the game.

A Paul O'Connell leap at the lineout inside his own half lead to a lung bursting Tommy Bowe gallop into French territory. O'Connell was on hand to handle following a ruck, before O'Gara found Heaslip on the 22 and the Number 8 produced a searing, weaving run that took him between two French tight forwards, followed by a sublime step off the left foot to charge over the French line to record Ireland's first try of the campaign to the delight of the home faithful.

O'Gara converted and the game looked to be turning Ireland's way as the men in green grasped the initiative for the first time in the match. If the French were rattled, they weren't showing it and straight from the restart it was Ireland's turn to do some back-pedalling as the hirsute Sebastian Chabal charged at the Irish defence. It came to nothing, however, as the Irish defence held firm.

On the stroke of half-time, Lionel Beauxis struck a drop-goal which saw the teams troop off down the tunnel with Ireland's lead now down to a mere three points. Half-time: Ireland 13 France 10.

Ireland blasted out of the traps at the start of the second half and there was a mere three minutes on the clock when O'Driscoll brushed past Beauxis' half-hearted tackle to score the kind of try which had been missing from the captain's armoury in recent times. That said he did produce a beautiful step inside to go over.

O'Gara's routine conversion extended the Irish lead to 20-10, providing the cushion of a two score lead for the first time in the contest and handing the initiative once again to Ireland in what was shaping up as a pulsating end to end battle between two juggernauts unwilling to forfeit the initiative.

Yet again, France regrouped and launched another attack as Harinordoquy pounced on some scrappy Irish play to set up an attack finished off by Medard's try. The French winger touched down after getting the luck of the bounce from Beauxis' chip over the home defence. Beauxis missed the conversion but his second drop-goal of the day cut Ireland's lead to 20-18. And there was still 23 minutes left. God!

To add further to the growing anxiety seeping into the great stadium, O'Gara missed a penalty from an angle. This was all too agonisingly familiar. But just as the match threatened to slip away from Ireland, they got up, dusted themselves off and started again, responding with a 66th minute punch that left the French reeling and from which they never recovered.

A forwards drive saw the home side move deep into French territory and the attack was finished off brilliantly by the twinkle toed replacement Gordon D'Arcy dancing his way over the line to celebrate his return to the international stage since breaking his arm in the opening game of the 2008 campaign.

O'Gara's conversion extended Ireland's lead to 27-18 but there was only a score between the teams when Beauxis landed a penalty four minutes from time to reduce the margin to a paltry six points. At that stage, memories of Vincent Cleric's late try that broke Irish hearts in 2007 was looming over Croke Park like a banshee.

O'Gara's immediate penalty eased home nerves just ever so slightly as the clock ticked agonisingly down. The final whistle brought an end to one of the greatest games ever seen in the championship.

Finally, after seven long years the nemesis had been slain and the optimism that enveloped Ireland all week was proved not to be misplaced.

If the Grand Slam itself was a monkey on Ireland's back that needed slaying then this was a chimpanzee that needed decapitating and one that gave Ireland's followers, ravenous and starved of success, real cause for optimism. Once again we dared to dream: Could this really be our year? Only time would tell.

After the earlier anaemic encounter at Twickenham, in which England defeated a poor Italian side 36-11 this contest lit up the Six Nations and the 80,000 plus crowd in Dublin as Ireland claimed their first win in eight attempts against the French.

Wales's routine victory over a pedestrian Scotland at Hampden Park the following day saw the reigning Champions retain their favourite's status at 5/4 with Ireland now firm second favourites at 2/1.

"I didn't show a lot of emotion but I admit this time it was there, inside me. It was a very special day in my life. I came here for different experiences; this is the sort of experience I wanted. I had such great moments coaching in South Africa. This was certainly up there with them." Gert Smal.

So it's Au revoir France and Ciao Italia.

Ireland: Kearney, Bowe, B. O'Driscoll (capt), P. Wallace, Fitzgerald, O'Gara, O'Leary, Horan, Flannery, Hayes, O'Callaghan, O'Connell, Ferris, D. Wallace and Heaslip.

Replacements: R. Best for Flannery (49), Court, O'Kelly, Stringer, D'Arcy for Wallace (63), Murphy for Kearney (79), Leamy for Ferris (79).

Not Used: Court, O'Kelly and Stringer.

France: Poitrenaud, Malzieu, Fritz, Jauzion, Medard, Beauxis, Tillous-Borde, Faure, Szarzewski, Lecouls, Chabal, Nallet; Dusautoir, Ouedraogo and Harinordoquy.

Replacements: Kayser for Szarzewski (58), Mas for Lecouls (40), Millo-Chluski for Chabal (62), Picamoles for Harinordoquy (71), Parra for Tillous-Borde (68)

Not Used: Baby and Heymans.

Att: 82,000

Referee: N Owens (Wales).

Match Stats:

IRELAND:

Scoring –

Tries:	3
Conversions:	3/3
Penalty Goals:	3/5
Drop Goals:	0/0

Phases Of Play –

Scrums Won:	9
Scrums Lost:	0
Lineouts Won:	8
Lineouts Lost:	1
Penalties Conceded:	2
Free-Kicks Conceded:	3
Mauls Won:	6
Ruck And Drive:	32
Ruck And Pass:	33

Ball Won –

In Open Play:	71
In Opponents' 22	12

At Set Pieces: 27

Turnovers Won: 4

Team Statistics –

Passes Completed: 103

Line Breaks: 4

Possession Kicked: 39

Errors From Kicks: 8

Kicks To Touch: 8

Kicks/Passes: 27%

Tackles Made: 95

Tackles Missed: 14

Tackle Completion: 87%

Offloads In Tackle: 4

Offloads/Tackled: 5%

Total Errors Made: 16

Errors/Ball Won: 16%

Minutes In Possession –

First Half: 15:27; Second Half: 16:57

Minutes In Opponents' Half –

First Half: 15:43; Second Half: 25:32

FRANCE:

Scoring –

Tries:	2
Conversions:	1/2
Penalty Goals:	1/1
Drop Goals:	2/2

Phases Of Play –

Scrums Won:	10
Scrums Lost:	0
Lineouts Won:	11
Lineouts Lost:	2
Penalties Conceded:	10
Free-Kicks Conceded:	0
Mauls Won:	3
Ruck And Drive:	15
Ruck And Pass:	61

Ball Won –

In Open Play:	79
In Opponents' 22	29
At Set Pieces:	23
Turnovers Won:	3

Team Statistics –

Passes Completed:	174
Line Breaks:	7
Possession Kicked:	29
Errors From Kicks:	6
Kicks To Touch:	3
Kicks/Passes:	14%
Tackles Made:	71
Tackles Missed:	5
Tackle Completion:	93%
Offloads In Tackle:	7
Offloads/Tackled:	7%
Total Errors Made:	16
Errors/Ball Won:	15%

Minutes In Possession –

First Half: 19:59; Second Half: 21:01

Minutes In Opponents' Half –

First Half: 29:12; Second Half: 21:07

Top Carries:

10 – Yannick Jauzion

8 – Julien Malzieu

7 – Imanol Harinordoquy, Dimitri Szarzewski

6 – David Wallace

Top Tacklers:

13 –Luke Fitzgerald

11 – Thierry Dusautoir

9 – David Wallace, Lionel Nallett, Paul O'Connell

Most Missed Tackles:

2 –Paul O'Connell, Ronan O'Gara, Paddy Wallace

1 – Brian O'Driscoll, Lionel Beauxis

Most Offloads:

2 – Julien Malzieu

1 – Stephen Ferris, Imanol Harinordoquy, Benjamin Kayser, Rob Kearney

Most Errors:

7 – Clement Poitrenaud

3 – Jamie Heaslip, Rob Kearney

2 – Thierry Dusautoir, Stephen Ferris

How they stood after Round 1

Round 1 Tables and results: 08/09 February 2009

Ireland	30	France	21
England	36	Italy	11
Scotland	13	Wales	26

	Played	Won	Drew	Lost	Points For	Against	points+/-	Points
Ireland	1	1	0	0	36	11	+25	2
Wales	1	1	0	0	26	13	+13	2
England	1	1	0	0	30	21	+9	2
France	1	0	0	1	21	30	-9	0
Scotland	1	0	0	1	19	26	-13	0
Italy	1	0	0	1	6	27	-25	0

Round 2
Sunday 15th February 2009
Italy vs Ireland

Declan Kidney kept faith with the team that beat France, naming an unchanged side for the second round clash with Italy at Stadio Flaminio in Rome.

Both Paddy Wallace and Jerry Flannery were passed fit after picking up injuries in the France game and prepared to take up their positions at centre and hooker.

Team captain Brian O'Driscoll was looking forward to earning his 90th cap as prop John Hayes prepared to equal the Irish cap record of 91 appearances of his fellow squad member Malcolm O'Kelly, while winger Tommy Bowe was set to represent his country for the 20th time.

IRELAND TEAM & REPLACEMENTS
(vs Italy, 2009 RBS Six Nations Championship, Stadio Flaminio, Sunday, February 15th,2009

15 - Robert Kearney (UCD – Leinster)

14 - Tommy Bowe (Ospreys)

13 - Brian O'Driscoll (UCD – Leinster) (capt)

12 - Paddy Wallace (Ballymena – Ulster)

11 - Luke Fitzgerald (Blackrock College – Leinster)

10 - Ronan O'Gara (Cork Constitution – Munster)

9 - Tomas O'Leary (Dolphin – Munster)

1 - Marcus Horan (Shannon – Munster)

2 - Jerry Flannery (Shannon – Munster)

3 - John Hayes (Bruff – Munster)

4 - Donncha O'Callaghan (Cork Constitution – Munster)

5 - Paul O'Connell (Young Munster – Munster)

6 - Stephen Ferris (Dungannon – Ulster)

7 - David Wallace (Garryowen – Munster)

8 - Jamie Heaslip (Naas – Leinster)

Replacements:

16 - Rory Best (Banbridge – Ulster)

17 - Tom Court (Malone – Ulster)

18 - Malcolm O'Kelly (St. Mary's College – Leinster)

19 - Denis Leamy (Cork Constitution – Munster)

20 - Peter Stringer (Shannon – Munster)

21 - Gordon D'Arcy (Lansdowne – Leinster)

22 - Geordan Murphy (Leicester)

Italy	(9) 9
Pens:	McLean (3)
Ireland	(14) 38

Tries: Bowe, Fitzgerald (2), D. Wallace, O'Driscoll Cons: O'Gara (4), Kearney Pen: O'Gara

First up for the weekend's second round of matches was France v Scotland. The Scotland side that turned up at the Stade De France bore little resemblance to the side blown away by Wales in the first round of matches. That said, despite a vastly improved performance, the Scots were outdone by their huge error count and some peculiar refereeing decisions; one of which saw the French (who ran out 22-13 winners, to notch up their first points of the campaign), awarded a try after what looked like a forward pass.

England also stepped up to the plate against Wales in Cardiff, following their flat performance against Italy. They actually outscored the Welsh by two tries to one but their indiscipline once again let them down as Wales notched up their eighth Six Nations victory in succession.

At the Stadio Flaminio, Ireland were shaken by Italy early on but eventually wore their hosts down and won at a canter, scoring five tries and conceding none to add further momentum to their growing Grand Slam ambitions.

Italy were fired up by the heavy criticism that greeted their 36-11 Twickenham horror show. But their passion could only take them so far.

They signalled their intentions early in the contest when Man of the Match Rob Kearney was the victim of a vicious clothes line tackle by Andrea Masi, which should have merited a red rather than the yellow that was shown to the Biarritz full-back. And as the match progressed one wondered if the body count would be greater than the points count. Both the blood bin and the sin bin were overworked.

A disjointed first half bereft of pattern or structure was strewn with unforced errors which played into the Italians' hands. Wallace was penalised for holding on, McLean booted Italy ahead on five minutes. Ten minutes later their lead was doubled as another McLean missile flew over. As they had done against France, Ireland had begun lethargically.

It was an impressive opening quarter from Italy, who were capitalising ruthlessly on Ireland's error-strewn display.

But they then paid a heavy price for a mistake of their own in the 19th minute when a promising attacking lineout was undone by a ponderous move in midfield which allowed Bowe to sneak in and intercept a pass destined for Mirco Bergamasco.

With Masi absent at full-back, Bowe, pursued by three Italian defenders, had a clear run to the line and crossed the whitewash with Kaine Robertson attached to his back. O'Gara added the conversion.

O'Gara's early kicking, hindered by the wind, was poor but Ireland were able to build a head of steam with Kearney, O'Connell and Ferris making ground.

O'Gara, wary of the blustery conditions, turned down two long-range shots at goal, usually within his reach, in favour of finding touch. Both attacking lineouts were picked apart by the wily Italians – Sergio Parisse catching the eye with one steal - before McLean landed another three points to restore the Italians lead.

Gonzalo Canale charged down a clearance by O'Gara and was then tackled without the ball by the Ireland fly-half, who, with five minutes of the half remaining, received a yellow card as punishment. Prop Salvatore Perugini joined O'Gara in the sin-bin for infringing at the lineout.

For all their possession and spirit, Nick Mallett's team never threatened the visitors' line, running out of ideas and steam after their barnstorming opening 35 minutes. And after five minutes on the rack Italy's line finally cracked on the stroke of half-time.

Fully 19 phases of play passed when Ferris surged forward and offloaded in the tackle to Fitzgerald, who dashed home from eight metres. In the absence of O'Gara, Kearney converted. Half-Time: Italy 9 Ireland 14.

The second half opened in much the same vein with Ireland pounding away at the home defence.

Heaslip almost crossed after running hard on to a Brian O'Driscoll offload but was hauled down inches short of the line.

Bowe then nearly wriggled over and once again the dogged Italian resistance was broken with David Wallace picking a path through the ragged Italian defence for a try converted by O'Gara.

It was a full 52 minutes into the contest when O'Gara landed his first penalty of the afternoon, taking Ireland into an unassailable 24-9 lead going into the final quarter. With the Azzurri offering little in attack, Ireland looked done and dusted.

Ireland seemed to have settled for the points and the game appeared to be petering out until they got a second wind in the dying minutes to breathe new life into a dying contest. Fitzgerald and Gordon D'Arcy combined at a quickly-taken lineout to send the former in and with two minutes to go O'Driscoll galloped the length of the field on the intercept for Ireland's fifth try of the match.

The match never achieved the high octane levels witnessed against France and the final two tries put something of a gloss on the score line. Ireland would have been disappointed by their failure to put the Azzurri to the sword in the second half which they dominated, a large error count preventing them from cutting loose. That said, for the second week in succession Ireland battened down the hatches and then took their chances. What was most impressive was the mental sharpness, the ability to take decisions and responsibility, of players like Bowe, Fitzgerald and Ferris – all from outside the 'senior' group – and Declan Kidney must get credit for creating the conditions which allowed these skills to develop.

Tactically, Ireland's efforts to run around the Italian blitz did not come off but a slight re-organisation and the adoption of a more conservative plan at half-time worked well.

Arrivederci Italia; bring on England!

Italy: Masi, Robertson, Canale, Micro Bergamasco, Pratichetti, McLean, Griffen, Perugini, Ongaro, Castrogiovanni, Dellape, Reato, Zanni, Mauro Bergamasco and Parisse.

Replacements: Bacchetti for Robertson (20), Garcia for Canale (48), Toniolatti for McLean (72), Festuccia for Ongaro (41), Nieto for Castrogiovanni (33), Del Fava for Dellape (48), Sole for Reato (48).

Sin Bin: Masi (1), Perugini (36).

Ireland: Kearney, Bowe, B. O'Driscoll, P. Wallace, Fitzgerald, O'Gara, O'Leary, Horan, Flannery, Hayes, O'Callaghan, O'Connell, Ferris, D. Wallace and Heaslip.

Replacements: D'Arcy for P. Wallace (41), Stringer for O'Leary (72), Court for Horan (55), Best for Flannery (60), O'Kelly for O'Connell (77), Leamy for Ferris (62), Murphy for Kearney (75).

Not Used:

Sin Bin: O'Gara (32).

Att: 30,000

Ref: C White (RFU).

Match Stats:

ITALY:

Scoring

Tries:	0
Conversions:	0/0
Penalty Goals:	3/4
Drop Goals:	0/0

Phases Of Play –

Scrums Won:	6
Scrums Lost:	0
Lineouts Won:	8
Lineouts Lost:	4
Penalties Conceded:	18
Free-Kicks Conceded:	2
Mauls Won:	0
Ruck And Drive:	6
Ruck And Pass:	35

Ball Won –

In Open Play:	41
In Opponents' 22	3

At Set Pieces: 26

Turnovers Won: 2

Team Statistics –

Passes Completed: 89

Line Breaks: 0

Possession Kicked: 18

Errors From Kicks: 2

Kicks To Touch: 3

Kicks/Passes: 16%

Tackles Made: 114

Tackles Missed: 19

Tackle Completion: 85%

Offloads In Tackle: 1

Offloads/Tackled: 2%

Total Errors Made: 6

Errors/Ball Won: 8%

Minutes In Possession –

First Half: 04:48;

Second Half: 09:28

Minutes In Opponents' Half –

First Half: 16:13

Second Half: 12:18

IRELAND:

Scoring –

Tries: 5

Conversions: 5/5

Penalty Goals: 1/1

Drop Goals: 0/0

Phases Of Play –

Scrums Won: 3

Scrums Lost: 0

Lineouts Won: 16

Lineouts Lost: 0

Penalties Conceded: 12

Free-Kicks Conceded: 0

Mauls Won: 5

Ruck And Drive: 23

Ruck And Pass: 70

Ball Won –

In Open Play:	98
In Opponents' 22	47
At Set Pieces:	37
Turnovers Won:	3

Team Statistics –

Passes Completed:	157
Line Breaks:	8
Possession Kicked:	15
Errors From Kicks:	3
Kicks To Touch:	5
Kicks/Passes:	8%
Tackles Made:	50
Tackles Missed:	4
Tackle Completion:	92%
Offloads In Tackle:	7
Offloads/Tackled:	6%
Total Errors Made:	10
Errors/Ball Won:	7%

Minutes In Possession –

First Half: 14:15;

Second Half: 11:14

Minutes In Opponents' Half –

First Half: 25:59;

Second Half: 31:16

Top Carries:

10 – Paul O'Connell

8 – Sergio Parisse

6 – David Wallace, Matteo Pratichetti

5 – Stephen Ferris

Top Tacklers:

16 – Mauro Bergamasco

15 – Alessandro Zanni

13 – Paul O'Connell

10 – Carlos Nieto

9 – Luke McLean

Most Missed Tackles:

3 – Matteo Pratichetti

2 – Paul Griffen, Mauro Bergamasco, Luke McLean, Mirco Bergamasco

Most Offloads:

3 – Paul O'Connell

1 – Brian O'Driscoll, Tommy Bowe, David Wallace, Ronan O'Gara

Most Errors:

2 – Jerry Flannery, Paul Griffen, Rob Kearney, Andrea Masi, Paul O'Connell

How they stood after Round 2

Round 2 Tables and results: 14/15 February 2009

France	22	Scotland	13
Wales	23	England	15
Italy	9	Ireland	38

	Played	Won	Drew	Lost	Points For	Against	points+/-	Points
Ireland	2	2	0	0	68	30	+30	4
Wales	2	2	0	0	49	28	+21	4
England	2	1	0	1	51	34	+17	2
France	2	1	0	1	43	43	0	2
Scotland	2	0	0	2	26	48	-22	0
Italy	2	0	0	2	20	74	-54	0

Round 3
Sunday 28th February 2009
Ireland vs England

Ireland, the Six Nations leaders, top of the pile ahead of Wales on points difference after running in nine tries against France and Italy, named an unchanged team for the third time in a row.

As well as consistency, the Irish also had longevity, as reflected in arguably the most-capped 22 in Test history. The starting XV and seven substitutes weighed in with an aggregate of almost 900 caps and it would have been closer to four figures had their most-capped player, Malcolm O'Kelly, not been omitted from the bench. Instead, John Hayes prepared to join the Leinster lock at the top of the all-time list by appearing in his 92nd Test, one more than Brian O'Driscoll and two ahead of Ronan O'Gara.

Six other players boasted more than a half-century of caps – the Munster quintet of Marcus Horan (63), Paul O'Connell (59), Donncha O'Callaghan (52), David Wallace (52) and reserve scrum-half Peter Stringer (87), plus the one English-based member of the 22, Leicester's long-serving full back-cum-wing Geordan Murphy (61).

The only selection issue, Paddy Wallace or Gordon D'Arcy at inside centre, resolved itself in favour of the former. Wallace hoped to go the distance after collecting 22 stitches in head injuries which forced him to make an early exit from both the French and Italian games.

Commenting on the injury Wallace said: "Maybe I should wear a motorcycle crash helmet or something. You expect the odd stitch over the course of the season but I've had 26 of them in next to no time, starting with four against Munster last month. The Italian one was really freakish. I got a knee in the back and then when Brian (O'Driscoll) came in to clear the ruck, I rolled into his fist."

IRELAND TEAM & REPLACEMENTS

(vs England, 2009 RBS Six Nations Championship, Croke Park, Saturday, February 28th, kick-off 5.30pm

15 - Robert Kearney (UCD – Leinster)

14 - Tommy Bowe (Ospreys)

13 - Brian O'Driscoll (UCD – Leinster) Captain

12 - Paddy Wallace (Ballymena – Ulster)

11 - Luke Fitzgerald (Blackrock College – Leinster)

10 - Ronan O'Gara (Cork Constitution – Munster)

9 - Tomas O'Leary (Dolphin – Munster)

1 - Marcus Horan (Shannon – Munster)

2 - Jerry Flannery (Shannon – Munster)

3 - John Hayes (Bruff – Munster)

4 - Donncha O'Callaghan (Cork Constitution – Munster)

5 - Paul O'Connell (Young Munster – Munster)

6 - Stephen Ferris (Dungannon – Ulster)

7 - David Wallace (Garryowen – Munster)

8 - Jamie Heaslip (Naas – Leinster)

Replacements:

16 - Rory Best (Banbridge – Ulster)

17 - Tom Court (Malone – Ulster)

18 - Mick O'Driscoll (Cork Constitution – Munster)

19 - Denis Leamy (Cork Constitution – Munster)

20 - Peter Stringer (Shannon – Munster)

21 - Gordon D'Arcy (Lansdowne – Leinster)

22 – Geordan Murphy (Leicester)

Ireland: (3) 14

Tries: O'Driscoll **Pens:** O'Gara (2) **Drop:** O'Driscoll

England: (3) 13

Try: Armitage **Con:** Goode **Pens:** Flood, Armitage

Before a ball was fought over in anger at Croker, one thing was clear: there was only one team left that could achieve the Grand Slam and there would be no back-to-back Slams for Wales.

Following Wales's defeat 21-16 in Paris in the first ever Friday night Six Nations game, Ireland now stood alone as the only undefeated nation in the competition. This is the sort of added pressure Ireland should relish ahead of the visit of England. At the other end of the table, Scotland recorded a 26-6 victory over Italy giving them their first points of the Championship.

The hype surrounding England's second and last visit to GAA HQ was almost muted in comparison to the hyperbole surrounding their 2007 visit. This time the talk was of the Grand Slam challenge rather than that of anthems and foreign games. There was also no talk of a red carpet for Martin Johnson – there just wasn't one. He did get a hot reception from the Croker faithful, who won't forgive him for getting Mary's shoes dirty.

Could the green machine handle what would surely be a third successive brutal encounter to keep the ever increasing dream of a clean sweep alive for another fortnight?

From the first whistle Ireland thundered into their opponents, scrapping for every inch, conscious that they were engaging in trench warfare. As a consequence, the opening salvos were, to say the least, untidy, dogged by spells of scrappy, unattractive play with possession continually being kicked away.

The closest Ireland got to breaking down a dogged England defence was when Thomas O'Leary's box kick caught Mark Cueto on the hop, before he recovered to prevent Tommy Bowe from touching down.

Ireland had the better of the possession but O'Gara was uncharacteristically wayward with two penalties before landing a third, which had its origins in O'Driscoll's cleverness after England had strayed offside in the 29th minute.

England applied a bit of pressure just before the break and got level with a simple Toby Flood penalty from close in front of the posts after some impressive spoiling from Nick Kennedy in the lineout. Half-time: Ireland 3 England 3.

The second half was a more enterprising affair, with the realisation dawning on Ireland that to win a game of this magnitude they would have to up the tempo, take greater risks and show more ambition.

Within a minute of the restart they won another kickable penalty only for O'Gara's effort to strike a post.

Five minutes later O'Driscoll lifted the Dublin crowd with an audacious 40 yard drop-goal: Ireland 6 England 3

But there was momentary concern for the Irish skipper after a nasty-looking clash of heads with Riki Flutey.

After treatment, O'Driscoll was able to continue, but the Leinster centre was soon flattened again by a late body check by Delon Armitage who escaped what should have been a yellow card.

Then came the game's defining moment. For six minutes Ireland laid siege to the England line and signalled their ambition by declining four penalty goal opportunities in favour of lineout ball. Although maybe that had more to do with Ronan's misfiring boot.

Under pressure, England were warned about infringements and former captain Vickery was sin-binned in the 55th minute for not allowing Ireland to release the ball quickly.

The home side remained camped yards from the try-line and O'Driscoll powered over, after six previous drives had fallen just short, in the 57th minute for a typically brave try- the skipper's 35th try in 91 Tests for Ireland – no need to guess what happened next – yup, O'Gara missed the conversion.

England tried to hit back quickly and a try looked on when replacement Mathew Tait made a darting break, only to be stopped in his tracks by a wonderfully timed Rob Kearney tackle with the try-line in sight.

Ninety seconds and three phases later a stray English pass went straight into touch. And Ireland survived.

England reduced the deficit to just five points when Armitage assumed the kicking duties from a punch-drunk Flood to land a well-struck penalty from long range. But, as against Italy and Wales in their previous two games, indiscipline once again cost England.

Replacement Care was given a yellow card after shoulder-charging Marcus Horan, with O'Gara rediscovering his kicking form to slide the penalty between the posts to put Ireland two scores ahead.

They needed it as two minutes from time a break from Tindall set up play in the Irish half which ended with an Armitage try which was converted by Goode.

It gave England a chance of stealing an unlikely victory but they ran out of time to mount another meaningful attack.

With Ronan O'Gara landing only two of his six kicks, Ireland were helped by the sin-binning of England prop Phil Vickery and scrum-half Danny Care.

England were left to rue that indiscipline after Delon Armitage's late try and Andy Goode's conversion.

So a relieved Ireland remained the only unbeaten side in the championship, on top of the pile with six points, followed by Wales and France on four each.

Ireland captain and Man of the Match after another heroic display, Brian O'Driscoll paid tribute to England: "I don't think people give England the credit they deserve. They are always a hard team. They have shown in previous games it's always hard to break them down and we found that to be the case."

That said it was now three from three with all lifelines remaining intact. It was now time to move on and prepare for a visit to Murrayfield.

Ireland: Kearney, Bowe, B O'Driscoll, P. Wallace, Fitzgerald, O'Gara, O'Leary, Horan, Flannery, Hayes, O'Callaghan, O'Connell, Ferris, D. Wallace, Heaslip.

Replacements: Stringer for O'Leary (65), Best for Flannery (68), Leamy for Heaslip (68). Not Used: Court, M O'Driscoll, D'Arcy, Murphy.

England: D. Armitage, Sackey, Tindall, Flutey, Cueto, Flood, Ellis, Sheridan, Mears, Vickery, Borthwick, Kennedy, Haskell, Worsley and Easter.

Replacements: Tait for Sackey (57), Goode for Flood (66), Care for Ellis (58), White for Sheridan (77), Hartley for Mears (66), Croft for Kennedy (69), Narraway for Easter (76).

Sin Bin: Vickery (55), Care (69).

Att: 82,000

Ref: Craig Joubert (South Africa).

Match Stats:

IRELAND:

Scoring –

Tries:	1
Conversions:	0/1
Penalty Goals:	2/5
Drop Goals:	1/2

Phases Of Play –

Scrums Won:	6
Scrums Lost:	0
Lineouts Won:	16
Lineouts Lost:	2
Penalties Conceded:	8
Free-Kicks Conceded:	0
Mauls Won:	4
Ruck And Drive:	26

Ruck And Pass: 50

Ball Won –

In Open Play: 80
In Opponents' 22   12
At Set Pieces: 38
Turnovers Won: 5

Team Statistics –

Passes Completed: 120
Line Breaks: 3
Possession Kicked: 42
Errors From Kicks: 3
Kicks To Touch: 6
Kicks/Passes: 25%
Tackles Made: 77
Tackles Missed: 2
Tackle Completion: 97%
Offloads In Tackle: 4
Offloads/Tackled: 4%
Total Errors Made: 11
Errors/Ball Won: 9%

Minutes In Possession –

First Half: 17:41;

Second Half: 19:01

Minutes In Opponents' Half –

First Half: 21:10;

Second Half: 31:01

ENGLAND:

Scoring –

Tries: 1

Conversions: 1/1

Penalty Goals: 2/2

Drop Goals: 0/0

Phases Of Play –

Scrums Won: 4

Scrums Lost: 0

Lineouts Won: 13

Lineouts Lost: 1

Penalties Conceded: 16

Free-Kicks Conceded: 2

Mauls Won: 2

Ruck And Drive:	11
Ruck And Pass:	47

Ball Won –

In Open Play:	60
In Opponents' 22	9
At Set Pieces:	25
Turnovers Won:	1

Team Statistics –

Passes Completed:	138
Line Breaks:	3
Possession Kicked:	37
Errors From Kicks:	3
Kicks To Touch:	7
Kicks/Passes:	21%
Tackles Made:	89
Tackles Missed:	5
Tackle Completion:	94%
Offloads In Tackle:	8
Offloads/Tackled:	10%
Total Errors Made:	9
Errors/Ball Won:	10%

Minutes In Possession –

First Half: 12:08;

Second Half: 11:26

Minutes In Opponents' Half –

First Half: 20:23

Second Half: 18:26

Top Carries:

7 – Paul O'Connell, Mike Tindall

6 – Nick Easter

5 – Mark Cueto

4 – David Wallace

Top Tacklers:

15 – Joe Worsley

10 – Stephen Ferris, James Haskell

9 – Steve Borthwick, Paul O'Connell

Most Missed Tackles:

2 – Joe Worsley

1 – Brian O'Driscoll, Nick Easter, Jamie Heaslip, Paddy Wallace

<u>Most Offloads:</u>

2 – Joe Worsley

1 – Danny Care, Mark Cueto, Stephen Ferris, Andy Goode

<u>Most Errors:</u>

3 – Stephen Ferris, Ronan O'Gara

2 – Luke Fitzgerald, Tomas O'Leary

1 – Delon Armitage

How they stood after Round 3

France	21	Wales	16
Scotland	26	Italy	6
Ireland	14	England	13

	Played	Won	Drew	Lost	Points For	Against	points+/-	Points
Ireland	3	3	0	0	82	43	+39	6
Wales	3	2	0	1	65	49	+16	4
England	3	2	0	1	64	59	+5	4
France	3	1	0	2	64	48	+16	2
Scotland	3	1	0	2	52	54	-2	2
Italy	3	0	0	3	26	100	-74	0

Round 4
Saturday 14th March 2009
Scotland vs Ireland

And so it was off to Murrayfield for round 4 and what someone once described as squeaky bum time. The realisation that Ireland had not lost to Scotland since the 2001 RBS Six Nations clash at Murrayfield and had outscored the Scots by 224 points to 97 in seven meetings since then, eased Irish nerves a little and stoked the fires of optimism just a little bit more.

Declan Kidney made four changes to the starting team that had seen of the challenge of England.

Gordon D'Arcy, Peter Stringer, Rory Best and Denis Leamy were all elevated to the starting line-up after several appearances from the replacements bench during the first three games. Their strong showings for their provinces in the Magners League during the break did their claims for starting berths no harm at all.

D'Arcy was set to start his first game for Ireland in over a year after being named at inside centre, in place of Paddy Wallace, who moved to the replacements bench.

Stringer took up the Number 9 jersey after swapping places with Thomas O'Leary, who had started the games against France, Italy and England.

The other two changes to the Ireland side were in the pack. In the front row, Best was named at hooker with Jerry Flannery taking Best's position amongst the replacements.

Leamy, who came on in place of Jamie Heaslip during the England game, was picked to start the game at Number 8 with Heaslip providing the cover this time around.

The game marked a significant milestone in the career of tighthead prop John Hayes, who was due to become the most capped Irish player of all time with 93 caps to his name, overhauling the previous record holder Malcolm O'Kelly.

IRELAND TEAM & REPLACEMENTS
(vs Scotland, 2009 RBS Six Nations Championship, Murrayfield, Saturday, March 14th, kick-off 5.30pm

15 - Robert Kearney (UCD – Leinster)

14 - Tommy Bowe (Ospreys)

13 - Brian O'Driscoll (UCD – Leinster) (capt)

12 - Gordon D'Arcy (Lansdowne – Leinster)

11 - Luke Fitzgerald (Blackrock College – Leinster)

10 - Ronan O'Gara (Cork Constitution – Munster)

9 - Peter Stringer (Shannon – Munster)

1 - Marcus Horan (Shannon – Munster)

2 - Rory Best (Banbridge – Ulster)

3 - John Hayes (Bruff – Munster)

4 - Donncha O'Callaghan (Cork Constitution – Munster)

5 - Paul O'Connell (Young Munster – Munster)

6 - Stephen Ferris (Dungannon – Ulster)

7 - David Wallace (Garryowen – Munster)

8 - Denis Leamy (Cork Constitution – Munster)

Replacements:

16 - Jerry Flannery (Shannon – Munster)

17 - Tom Court (Malone – Ulster)

18 - Mick O'Driscoll (Cork Constitution – Munster)

19 - Jamie Heaslip (Naas – Leinster)

20 - Tomas O'Leary (Dolphin – Munster)

21 - Paddy Wallace (Ballymena – Ulster)

22 - Geordan Murphy (Leicester)

Scotland (12) 15

Pens: Paterson 5

Ireland (9) 22

Tries: Heaslip **Cons:** O'Gara **Pens:** O'Gara 4 **Drops:** O'Gara

Wales' arrogance in dropping nine first choice players against Italy almost did for them in Rome, but for a single lapse in concentration that allowed Tom Jenkins to go over, Ireland might well have been looking at a Championship decider in Murrayfield and not in Cardiff as was widely predicted.

The pressure of a potential Grand Slam seemed to be weighing heavily on Irish shoulders in the first half at Murrayfield, while a fired-up Scotland came out determined to record only their second win of the campaign.

Early on they were passionate and gutsy, playing at a high tempo and dominating possession. Deservedly the hosts drew first blood with a Chris Paterson penalty on six minutes; O'Gara replied four minutes later to bring the scores level. Two more penalties from Patterson allowed Scotland to edge into a 9-3 lead after 20 minutes.

Ireland were warming up though, and when another penalty came their way just before the half hour, following a period of pressure, O'Gara slotted the kick to overtake England's Jonny Wilkinson as the leading points scorer in Five/Six Nations history.

O'Gara, back on track again after missing four of six kicks against England in Dublin, moved to 481 points, with Wilkinson on 479 and Wales' retired kicker Neil Jenkins on 406.

The turbulent, slightly scrappy, opening continued and Scotland went six points clear when Ireland prop John Hayes was penalised for taking a backward step to wheel a scrum.

But Scotland gifted the three points straight back from the kick-off when Jason White fumbled his catch and John Barclay caught the ball offside.

In the fading minutes of the half, Scotland went close to scoring the game's first try when Thom Evans countered from his own half. The left wing gathered his own chip-ahead and stepped past O'Gara before offloading to the supporting Phil Godman, but the fly-half was thundered into touch by a retreating Brian O'Driscoll just a few metres short of the Irish line.

And so the half ended with Ireland trailing their hosts 12-9. Those Irish fans with long memories were trying hard to remember a time when Ireland recovered from a losing half-time position to win a game. At this juncture history was not on Ireland's side. The last time it happened was actually nine years previously when, on a memorable day in Paris in March 2000, a hat trick of tries from a callow Brian O'Driscoll saw Ireland recover from a 13-7 half-time deficit to record a memorable 25-27 victory – Ireland's first in Paris for 28 years. That was then though and this was now.

Although Scotland had shown more energy in the first period, it was Ireland who came out with more vigour after the break, however, and they were putting the home side under increasing pressure.

The Scottish lineout particularly was creaking and under fire coach Frank Hadden replaced White with the fit-again Nathan Hines after just ten minutes of the second half.

But from the very next lineout Ireland scrum-half Peter Stringer took a quick tap off the top and scampered through a Scottish defence that opened up like the Red Sea, before offloading to Heaslip, a first-half replacement for Number 8 Denis Leamy, to crash over.

O'Gara converted and then stroked the 13th drop goal of his international career through the posts shortly after to create some daylight before Paterson's fifth penalty narrowed the gap to four points. 64 minutes on the clock: Scotland 12 Ireland 16.

The Irish fly-half missed his first kick on 68 minutes but made amends with a mere five minutes left to take Ireland to a precious converted try in front. Such was Ireland's superiority in the last quarter that the gap looked like a chasm.

Scotland seemed to sense the match was slipping away, and though they battled to keep Ireland out for the remainder of the match, the visitors were always on the front foot and were preparing for the march to Cardiff with history beckoning.

Ireland had also risen to fourth in the IRB World Rankings, their highest position for nearly two years.

France, who were still in the mix, collapsed against England at Twickenham in the weekend's last game to leave just two runners for the Championship: Ireland and Wales.

And so the dream of a first Grand Slam for 61 years remained alive and well. It was now within reach. It was now permitted to talk about the Wales game. Unbeaten Ireland led the RBS Six Nations table by two points from Wales. This was the deal: Wales needed to beat Ireland by 13 points at the Millennium Stadium to win the title. Only Ireland could win the Grand Slam. The hand of history was reaching out tantalisingly towards the men in green. And history, at the Millennium Stadium at least, was on Ireland's side!

Scotland: Paterson, Danielli, M. Evans, Morrison, T. Evans, Godman, Blair, Dickinson, Ford, Murray, White, Hamilton, Strokosch, Barclay and Taylor.

Replacements: De Luca for Morrison (70), Cusiter for Blair (51), Hall for Ford (57), Hines for White (50), Gray for Barclay (67).

Not Used: Low and Southwell.

Ireland: Kearney, Bowe, B. O'Driscoll, D'Arcy, Fitzgerald, O'Gara, Stringer, Horan, Best, Hayes, O'Callaghan, O'Connell, Ferris, D. Wallace and Leamy.

Replacements: Murphy for Kearney (75), O'Leary for Stringer (65), Flannery for Best (61), Heaslip for Leamy (30).

Not Used: Court, M. O'Driscoll and P. Wallace.

Att: 55,000

Ref: J Kaplan (South Africa).

Match Stats:

Scotland:

Scoring –

Tries:	0
Conversions:	0/0
Penalty Goals:	5/5
Drop Goals:	0/0

Phases Of Play –

Scrums Won:	3
Scrums Lost:	0
Lineouts Won:	12
Lineouts Lost:	4
Penalties Conceded:	8
Free-Kicks Conceded:	4
Mauls Won:	1
Ruck And Drive:	12
Ruck And Pass:	41

Ball Won –

In Open Play:	54
In Opponents' 22:	3
At Set Pieces:	26
Turnovers Won:	4

Team Statistics –

Passes Completed:	130
Line Breaks:	0
Possession Kicked:	25
Errors From Kicks:	5
Kicks To Touch:	5
Kicks/Passes:	16%

Tackles Made:	118
Tackles Missed:	9
Tackle Completion:	92%
Offloads In Tackle:	5
Offloads/Tackled:	6%
Total Errors Made:	17
Errors/Ball Won:	21%

Minutes In Possession –

First Half:	11:43;
Second Half:	11:19

Minutes In Opponents' Half –

First Half:	23:49;
Second Half:	12:23

IRELAND:

Scoring

Tries:	1
Conversions:	1/1
Penalty Goals:	4/5
Drop Goals:	1/2

Phases Of Play –

Scrums Won: 5

Scrums Lost: 0

Lineouts Won: 11

Lineouts Lost: 2

Penalties Conceded: 11

Free-Kicks Conceded: 1

Mauls Won: 2

Ruck And Drive: 31

Ruck And Pass: 73

Ball Won –

In Open Play: 106

In Opponents' 22: 29

At Set Pieces: 26

Turnovers Won: 7

Team Statistics –

Passes Completed: 191

Line Breaks: 1

Possession Kicked: 38

Errors From Kicks: 4

Kicks To Touch: 9

Kicks/Passes: 16%

Tackles Made:	72
Tackles Missed:	6
Tackle Completion:	92%
Offloads In Tackle:	3
Offloads/Tackled:	2%
Total Errors Made:	12
Errors/Ball Won:	9%

Minutes In Possession –

First Half:	11:19;
Second Half:	14:00

Minutes In Opponents' Half –

First Half:	15:01;
Second Half:	29:12

Top Carries:

9 – Gordon D'Arcy, Rob Kearney, Brian O'Driscoll

6 – Stephen Ferris, Luke Fitzgerald

Top Tacklers:

14 – Strokosch

11 – Taylor

9 – Dickinson, Murray

8 – M Evans

Most Missed Tackles:

2 – Godman, Morrison

1 – D'Arcy, Danielli, Ferris

Most Offloads:

2 – Darcy

1 – Danielli, Fitzgerald, Godman, M Evans

Most Errors:

4 – Godman

3 – O'Driscoll

2 – Danielli, Fitzgerald, T H Evans

How they stood after Round 4

Round 4 Tables and results: 14/15 March 2009

Italy	15	Wales	20
Scotland	15	Ireland	22
England	34	France	10

	Played	Won	Drew	Lost	Points For	Against	points+/-	Points
Ireland	4	4	0	0	104	58	+46	8
Wales	4	3	0	0	85	64	+21	6
England	4	2	0	2	98	58	+30	4
France	4	2	0	2	74	93	-19	4
Scotland	4	1	0	3	67	76	-9	2
Italy	4	0	0	4	41	120	-79	0

Round 5
Saturday 21st March 2009
Wales vs Ireland

Ireland last lost to Wales in Cardiff in 1983, then went on a run of victories in the Welsh capital that lasted extraordinarily until 2005 when they lost a championship showdown in the Millennium Stadium – one defeat in over a quarter of a century boded well. And that is not to mention two Heineken Cup wins for Munster; both in Cardiff and under the guiding hand of one Declan Kidney.

On the flip side, Wales needed to win by a 13 point margin to win the Championship and deny Ireland a rare Grand Slam. Cast your mind back to 1969 when a Wales victory over Ireland by a 13 point margin denied Ireland a Grand Slam. Would history repeat itself?

Here are the men that Declan Kidney put his trust in to clinch the elusive Grand Slam:

Peter Stringer dropped to the bench and Tomas O'Leary was recalled, whilst Jamie Heaslip and Jerry Flannery also returned.

IRELAND TEAM & REPLACEMENTS
(vs Wales, 2009 RBS Six Nations
Championship, Millennium Stadium, Saturday,
March 21st, kick-off 5.30pm

15 - Robert Kearney (UCD – Leinster)

14 - Tommy Bowe (Ospreys)

13 - Brian O'Driscoll (UCD – Leinster) (capt)

12 - Gordon D'Arcy (Lansdowne – Leinster)

11 - Luke Fitzgerald (Blackrock College – Leinster)

10 - Ronan O'Gara (Cork Constitution – Munster)

9 - Tomas O'Leary (Dolphin – Munster)

1 - Marcus Horan (Shannon – Munster)

2 - Jerry Flannery (Shannon – Munster)

3 - John Hayes (Bruff – Munster)

4 - Donncha O'Callaghan (Cork Constitution – Munster)

5 - Paul O'Connell (Young Munster – Munster)

6 - Stephen Ferris (Dungannon – Ulster)

7 - David Wallace (Garryowen – Munster)

8 - Jamie Heaslip (Naas – Leinster)

Replacements:

16 - Rory Best (Banbridge – Ulster))

17 - Tom Court (Malone – Ulster)

18 - Mick O'Driscoll (Cork Constitution – Munster)

19 - Denis Leamy (Cork Constitution – Munster)

20 - Peter Stringer (Shannon – Munster)

21 - Paddy Wallace (Ballymena – Ulster)

22 - Geordan Murphy (Leicester)

Wales (6) 15

Pens: S Jones 4 **Drop-goal:** S Jones

Ireland (0) 17

Try: Bowe, O'Driscoll **Cons:** O'Gara 2 **Drop-goal:** O'Gara

In the final day's undercard France brushed Italy aside, running in seven tries in a 50-8 mauling and England retained the Calcutta Cup with a 26-12 victory over Scotland at Twickenham.

Before the main event Wales' boss Warren Gatland upped the ante by saying that the Wales players nurture a genuine dislike of their Irish counterparts. O'Driscoll replied as only he can: "I don't personally have anything to say about it," he said. "They can show their dislike on the pitch and we'll show them the respect they deserve."

The hosts, needing to win by 13 points to retain their title, planned to target O'Gara from the outset. Wales skipper Ryan Jones set the tone and a bad example with a trip on the Irish fly-half with barely a minute on the clock.

Ireland lock Donncha O'Callaghan, as is his wont, objected to Jones's actions and a minor tussle between the players ensued, earning an early warning from English referee Wayne Barnes. From the resulting penalty, O'Gara failed from distance. Here we go again?

Ireland responded immediately with a Gordon D'Arcy break, only for Gavin Henson's tackle to thwart Luke Fitzgerald, followed by a testing O'Gara cross-kick that Shane Williams and Lee Byrne failed to deal with.

The pressure on Wales was relieved when Ian Gough's challenge knocked the ball out of Jerry Flannery's hands and Henson sent a huge clearance kick downfield.

The relief was short-lived however and at Wales first defensive lineout, the men in red looked in danger of cracking as Matthew Rees's throw could not be cleanly gathered and Shane Williams rescued his side, conceding a five-metre scrum in the process.

Wales held firm in defence, Mark Jones's tackle on Ireland captain O'Driscoll forced him to knock-on in a passage of play that led referee Barnes to warn both captains about off-the-ball incidents.

O'Gara kicked the ball out on the full twice, perhaps indicating the early attention Wales paid to him was paying dividends.

As ever, Paul O'Connell led the way as Ireland stole home lineout ball on successive occasions and as both sides belied the occasion to vary their attacking play, that advantage boosted the visitors' confidence.

The Grand Slam chasers were happy to kick for touch in the belief they could successfully attack Wales' lineout.

But after Lee Byrne departed with an ankle injury, Henson switched to full-back to accommodate Jamie Roberts. Denis Leamy then held on too long in a tackle on Martyn Williams at the back of a lineout and Stephen Jones kicked the 33rd minute penalty to draw first blood for Wales.

Another throw to Williams at the back spelled danger for Wales as the veteran flanker was unable to gather, but Fitzgerald blocked the defence from tackling O'Gara and Jones struck from 49 metres to give Wales a 6-0 lead going into the break.

Half-time: Wales 6 Ireland 0

Ireland began the second half with a Bowe burst down the right from an O'Driscoll pass, and an O'Gara cross-kick that Mark Jones made safe, but failed to mark before he stepped into touch.

That gave Ireland the platform and territory their forwards craved and after a series of close-quarter drives, O'Driscoll's good leg strength and body angle was enough for him to claim a 44th minute score that appeared to be seen by no one but the referee. And it took French television match official Romain Poite to confirm Wayne Barnes judgement. Two minutes later there was no requirement for debate as Tommy Bowe claimed O'Gara's chip and raced away from the pursuing Shane Williams to score under the posts.

O'Gara converted both tries to give Ireland a 14-6 lead. Plain sailing from here on in then? No.

O'Callaghan's petulant push on Mike Phillips after the scrum-half had knocked on gave fly-half Jones the chance to reduce the deficit, which he did, albeit via an upright. Just five in it now.

14-9.

A timely O'Driscoll tackle on Tom Shanklin helped thwart a Wales attack and Bowe was denied by a knock-on as he won an aerial joust with Ospreys team-mate Williams.

The other aerial battle, at the lineouts, was also going in Ireland's direction. But Irish composure once again failed them and Jones kicked his fourth penalty from the same amount of attempts. Only two in it now! 14-12.

Ahead of the final quarter, Wales coach Warren Gatland attempted to solve his side's lineout issues by sending Luke Charteris on for Gough and Huw Bennett for hooker Matthew Rees.

On 68 minutes Wales had the chance to take the lead. But Henson's rare long-range effort fell short. Soon after, Ireland brought on Peter Stringer at scrum-half for O'Leary for the final 10 minutes.

And that is when the drama truly unfolded. For the first time in the game, Wales' strike runners began to make their mark.

With five minutes remaining, wing Williams slipped to end one attack, but after Phillips' thunderous charge through the Irish defence, Jones dropped the goal that sent the Millennium Stadium into raptures of delight and looked to have won the Triple Crown for Wales. Three minutes left: Wales 15 Ireland 14 and yet another Irish Grand Slam dream looked, if not dead in the water, like it was certainly struggling for breath.

Moments later, on 78 minutes, Ireland went ahead through a Ronan O'Gara drop-kick, only to concede a penalty in injury time.

After 61 years of waiting, it came down to the last two seconds and the last two metres of the last game of the Championship as Stephen Jones had one last chance to redeem the season for Wales. His effort, from 48 metres, just inside the Ireland half, seemed to hang in the air for an eternity but fell just short of the posts. The heist was completed and Ireland were at last able to taste Grand Slam champagne. The long, tortuous journey to the Holy Grail had finally been completed and the Ireland Rugby class of 2009 completed the greatest achievement in Irish rugby history.

Wales, from being within two minutes of denying Ireland a Grand Slam, and their first ever Six-Nations title, suddenly had to come to terms with finishing fourth in the championship.

"Just when you thought you had seen all that there is to see in sport, along comes a game so nerve shredding, unbearably exciting that it will never be forgotten by those who were lucky enough to witness it," said David Walsh in the *Sunday Times*.

The riveting spectacle was unrelentingly brutal, occasionally brilliant and intensely fascinating.

In the words of Anne Robinson: "Ireland you win the Championship, Triple Crown and the Grand Slam; Wales you leave with nothing!"

Wales: Byrne; M. Jones, Shanklin, Henson, S. Williams, S. Jones, Phillips, Jenkins, Rees, A. Jones, Gough, A. Jones, D. Jones, M. Williams, R. Jones (capt.).

Replacements: Roberts for Byrne (30), Bennett for Rees (55), Charteris for Gough (55).

Not Used: Yapp, J. Thomas, Fury and Hook.

Ireland: Kearney, Bowe, B. O'Driscoll, D'Arcy, Fitzgerald; O'Gara, O'Leary, Horan, Flannery, Hayes, O'Callaghan, O'Connell, Ferris, D, Wallace and Heaslip.

Replacements: Murphy for Kearney (66), P. Wallace for Fitzgerald (76), Stringer for O'Leary (69), Best for Flannery (68), Leamy for Ferris (blood, 7), Court for Hayes (blood, 27).

Not Used: M. O'Driscoll.

Att: 74,625

Ref: Wayne Barnes (RFU).

Match Stats

WALES:

Scoring –

Tries:	0
Conversions:	0/0
Penalty Goals:	4/6
Drop Goals:	1/1

Phases Of Play –

Scrums Won:	5
Scrums Lost:	0
Lineouts Won:	16
Lineouts Lost:	6
Penalties Conceded:	5
Free-Kicks Conceded:	1
Mauls Won:	0
Ruck And Drive:	19
Ruck And Pass:	46

Ball Won –

In Open Play:	65
In Opponents' 22:	5
At Set Pieces:	36
Turnovers Won:	3

Team Statistics –

Passes Completed:	132
Line Breaks:	5
Possession Kicked:	26
Errors From Kicks:	2
Kicks To Touch:	1
Kicks/Passes:	16%

Tackles Made:	86
Tackles Missed:	11
Tackle Completion:	88%
Offloads In Tackle:	6
Offloads/Tackled:	7%
Total Errors Made:	12
Errors/Ball Won:	11%

Minutes In Possession –

First Half:	12:41;
Second Half:	09:16

Minutes In Opponents' Half –

First Half:	16:41;
Second Half:	18:12

IRELAND:

Scoring –

Tries:	2
Conversions:	2/2
Penalty Goals:	0/1
Drop Goals:	1/1

Phases Of Play –

Scrums Won:	6
Scrums Lost:	0
Lineouts Won:	9
Lineouts Lost:	1
Penalties Conceded:	15
Free-Kicks Conceded:	1
Mauls Won:	3
Ruck And Drive:	34
Ruck And Pass:	48

Ball Won –

In Open Play:	85
In Opponents'22:	36
At Set Pieces:	20
Turnovers Won:	5

Team Statistics –

Passes Completed:	127
Line Breaks:	5
Possession Kicked:	40
Errors From Kicks:	2
Kicks To Touch:	6
Kicks/Passes:	23%

Tackles Made: 81

Tackles Missed: 17

Tackle Completion: 82%

Offloads In Tackle: 4

Offloads/Tackled: 4%

Total Errors Made: 12

Errors/Ball Won: 11%

Minutes In Possession –

First Half: 11:21;

Second Half: 14:12

Minutes In Opponents' Half –

First Half: 24:28;

Second Half: 24:31

Top Carries:

9 - Brian O'Driscoll

8 - David Wallace, Stephen Jones

7 - Mike Phillips

6 - Alun Wyn Jones

Top Tacklers:

14 - Alun Wyn Jones

11 - Ian Gough

9 - Dafydd Jones, Martyn Williams

8 - Jerry Flannery

Most Missed Tackles:

3 - Ronan O'Gara

2 – Ian Gough, Gavin Henson, Marcus Horan, Paul O'Connell

Most Offloads:

2 - Brian O'Driscoll, Stephen Jones

1 - Dafydd Jones, Luke Fitzgerald, Gavin Henson

Most Errors:

2 - Lee Byrne, Paul O'Connell, Ronan O'Gara, Matthew Rees, Stephen Jones

Final Championship Table

Round 5 Tables and results: 21st March 2009

France	50	Italy	8
England	26	Scotland	12
Wales	15	Ireland	17

	Played	Won	Drew	Lost	Points For	Against	points +/-	Points
Ireland	5	5	0	0	121	73	+48	10
Wales	5	3	0	2	124	70	+54	6
England	5	3	0	2	124	101	+23	6
France	5	3	0	2	100	81	+19	6
Scotland	5	1	0	4	79	102	-23	2
Italy	5	0	0	5	49	170	-121	0

Appendix (i)

IRISH INTERNATIONAL APPEARANCE RECORDS
To March 2009

Best, Rory (34)

2005-06: NZ, A, W.

2006-07: A (2), SA, PI, W, F, E, S, It

2007-08: S, It (2), Na, Ge, Ar, F, S, W, E, NZ, A

2008-09: C (2), NZ, Ar, F, It, E, S, W, US.

Bowe, Tommy (23)

2004-05: Us, J (2)

2005-06: NZ, A, R, It, F.

2006-07: A.

2007-08: S (2), W, E, NZ, A

2008-09: C, NZ, Ar, F, It, E, S, W.

Court, Tom (4)

2008-09: It, C, W, Us.

D'Arcy, Gordon (41)

1999-00: R.

2002-03: Fi, Tg, Sam.

2003-04: F, W (2), E, It, S, SA.

2004-05: It.

2005-06: NZ (3), A , Ro, It, F, W, S, E.

2006-07: A (2), SA, PI, W, F, E, S, It

2007-08: It (2), Na, Ge, Ar, F.

2008-09: F, It, S, W.

Dempsy, Girvan (82)

1998-99: G, SA, F, E, S, It.

1999-00: A, E, S, It, F, W.

2000-01: SA, It, F, S, E, W.

2001-02: NZ (3), W, E, S, It, F.

2002-03: Ro, Ru, G, A, Ar, S, E, Sam.

2003-04: A (2), W (2), It, S (2), Ro, Na, Ar, F (2), E, It, SA (2).

2004-05: SA, Us, Ar, It, S, E, F, W, J (2).

2005-06: NZ (3), Ro, E.

2006-07: A (2), SA, PI, W, F, E, S, It

2007-08: It (2), Na, Ge, F (2), A.

2008-09: NZ.

Earls, Keith (2)

2008-09: C, NZ

Ferris, Stephen (13)

2006-07: Ar (2), PI.

2007-08: S, A.

2008-09: C, NZ, Ar, F, It, E, S, W.

Fitzgerald, Luke (12)

2006-07: PI, Ar.

2007-08: W, E.

2008-09: C, NZ, Ar, F, It, E, S, W.

Flannery, Jerry (31)

2005-06: R, It, F, W, S, E, NZ (2).

2006-07: A, W, F, E, S, It, Ar.

2007-08: S, It , Na, Ge, F, Ar, NZ, A.

2008-09: C, NZ, Ar, F, It, E, S, W.

Hayes, John (94)

1999-00: S, It, F, W, Ar, C.

2000-01: J, SA, It, F, R, S, W, E.

2001-02: Sam, NZ (3), W, E, S, It, F.

2002-03: Ro, Ru, G, A, Fi, Ar, S, It, F, W, E.

2003-04: Ro, Na, Ar, A, F (2), W, E, It, S, SA (2).

2004-05: SA, Us, Ar, It, S, E, F, W.

2005-06: NZ (3), A, Ro, It, F, W, S, E.

2006-07: A (2), SA, PI, W, F, E, S, It

2007-08: S (2), It (2), Na, Ge, F (2), Ar, W, E, NZ, A.

2008-09: C, NZ, Ar, F, It, E, S, W.

Heaslip, Jamie (18)

2006-07: PI, Ar.

2007-08: S (2), It, F, W, E, NZ, A.

2008-09: C, NZ, Ar, F, It, E, S, W.

Horan, Marcus (66)

1999-00: Us.

2002-03: Fi, Ar, S, It, F, W, E, Sam.

2003-04: A (2), It (2), S, Ro, Na, Ar, F, S, SA (2).

2004-05: SA, Us, It, S, E, F, W, J (2).

2005-06: NZ (3), A, Ro, It, W, S, E.

2006-07: A (2), SA, W, F, E, It

2007-08: It (2), Na, Ge, F (2), Ar, S, W, E, NZ, A.

2008-09: C, NZ, Ar, F, It, E, S, W.

Horgan, Shane (64)

1999-00: S, It, W, Ar, C.

2000-01: J, SA, It, S, W, E.

2001-02: NZ, S, It, F.

2002-03: A, Fi, Ar, S.

2003-04: Ro, Na, Ar, A, F (2), W, E, It, S, SA (2).

2004-05: SA, Us, Ar, It, S, E.

2005-06: NZ (3), A, Ro, It, F, W, S, E.

2006-07: A (2), SA, PI, F, E, S, It

2007-08: Ge, F, Ar, S, W, E, NZ, A.

2008-09: C.

Kearney, Rob (16)

2006-07: Ar.

2007-08: It, F, S, W, E, NZ, A.

2008-09: C, NZ, Ar, F, It, E, S, W.

Leamy, Denis (41)

2004-05: Us, It, J.

2005-06: NZ (3), A, Ro, It, F, W, S, E.

2006-07: A (2), SA, PI, W, F, E, S, It.

2007-08: It (2), Na, Ge, F (2), Ar, S, W, E, NZ, A.

2008-09: F, It, E, S, W, C, Us.

Murphy, Geordan (62)

1999-00: Us, C.

2000-01: J, R, S.

2001-02: Sam, NZ (2), W, E.

2002-03: Fi, S, It, F, W, E.

2003-04: A, W, It (2), S (2), SA.

2004-05: SA, Us, Ar, It, S, E, F, W.

2005-06: NZ (3), A, Ro, It, F, W, S, E.

2006-07: A (2), SA, W, F, Ar (2).

2007-08: S (2), It (2), Na, Ar, F, E, NZ, A.

2008-09: Ar, F, It, S, W.

O' Callaghan, Donncha (55)

2002-03: W, T, Sam.

2003-04: W, It, Ro, A, F, W, It, S, SA.

2004-05: Us, It, S, W.

2005-06: NZ (3), A, Ro, It, F, W, S, E.

2006-07: A (2), SA, PI, W, F, E, S, It.

2007-08: It (2), Na, Ge, F (2), Ar, S, W, E, NZ, A.

2008-09: C, NZ, Ar, F, It, E, S, W.

O'Connell, Paul (62)

2001-02: W, It, F, NZ.

2002-03: E, T, Sam.

2003-04: A, W, S, Ro, Na, Ar, A, F (2), W, E, S, SA (2).

2004-05: SA, Us, Ar, It, S, E, F, W.

2005-06: It, F, S, E, NZ (2).

2006-07: A (2), SA, PI, W, F, E, S.

2007-08: S (2), It , Na, Ge, F, Ar, W, E, NZ, A.

2008-09: C, NZ, Ar, F, It, E, S, W.

O'Driscoll, Brian (93)

1999-00: A (3) Ar (2) Us, Ro, E, S, It, F, W.

2000-01: J, SA, F, S, W, E.

2001-02: Sam, NZ (3), W, E, S, It, F.

2002-03: Ro, Ru, Ge, A, Fi, Ar, S, It, F, W, E.

2003-04: W, It, S (2), Ro, Na, Ar, A, F, W, E, It, SA (2).

2004-05: SA, Us, Ar, It, E, F, W.

2005-06: It, F, W, S, E, NZ (2).

2006-07: A (2), SA, PI, W, E, S, It.

2007-08: S(2), Na, Ge, F (2), Ar, It, W, NZ, A.

2008-09: C, NZ, Ar, F, It, E, S, W.

O'Driscoll, Mick (17)

2000-01: Ro.

2002-03: Fi.

2005-06: Ro, W, NZ (2).

2006-07: A, E, It, Ar (2).

2007-08: It, F, S, E.

2008-09: C, Us.

O'Gara, Ronan (92)

1999-00: S, It, F, W, Ar, Us, C.

2000-01: J, SA, It, F, S, W, E.

2001-02: Sam, W, E, S, It, F, NZ (2).

2002-03: Ro, Ru, Ge, A, Ar, W, E, T, Sam.

2003-04: A (2), S (2), W, Ro, Na, Ar, F (2), E, It, SA (2).

2004-05: SA, Ar, It, S, E, F, W.

2005-06: A, Ro, It, F, W, S, E, NZ (3).

2006-07: A (2), SA, PI, W, F, E, S, It.

2007-08: S (2), It (2), Na, Ge, F (2), Ar, W, E, NZ, A.

2008-09: C, NZ, Ar, F, It, E, S, W.

O'Kelly, Malcolm (92)

1997-98: NZ, C, It, S, F, W, E, SA (2).

1998-99: Ge, R, SA.

1999-00: A (3), Ar (3), Us (2), Ro, E, S, It, F, W.

2000-01: J, SA, It, F, S, W, E.

2001-02: NZ (3), E, S, It, F.

2002-03: Ro, Ru, Ge, A, Fi, Ar, S, It, F, W, E.

2003-04: A (2), W (2), S (2), Ro, Na, Ar, F (2), E, It, SA (2).

2004-05: SA, Ar, It, S, E, F, W.

2005-06: NZ, A, It, F, W, S, E.

2006-07: Ar (2), SA, PI, A.

2007-08: S, It (2), F (2), Ar.

2008-09: It.

O'Leary, Tomas (8)

2006-07: A.

2008-09: NZ, Ar, F, It, E, S, W.

Quinlan, Alan (27)

1999-00: Ro.

2000-01: It, F.

2001-02: NZ.

2002-03: Ru, Ge, A, Fi, Ar, S, It, F, W, E.

2003-04: A, W, Ro, Na, Ar, SA(2)

2004-05: J (2).

2006-07: Ar.

2007-08: S.

2008-09: C, NZ.

Stringer, Peter (91)

1999-00: S, It, F, W, Ar, C.

2000-01: J, SA, It, F, Ro, S, W, E.

2001-02: Sam, W, E, S, It, F, NZ (3).

2002-03: Ro, Ru, Ge, A, Ar, S, It, F, W, E.

2003-04: A (2), W (2), S (2), Ro, Na, Ar, F (2), E, It, SA (2).

2004-05: SA, Us, Ar, It, S, E, F, W, J (2).

2005-06: NZ (3), A, Ro, It, F, W, S, E.

2006-07: A (2), SA, PI, W, E, S, It.

2007-08: It (2), Na, Ge, S, E, NZ, A.

2008-09: C (2), It, E, S, W, Us.

Wallace, David (55)

1999-00: Ar, Us.

2000-01: It, F, Ro, S, W, E.

2001-02: NZ, W, E, S, It, F.

2002-03: T, Sam.

2003-04: W, S (2), SA (2).

2004-05: J.

2005-06: It, F, W, S, E, NZ (2).

2006-07: A (2), SA, W, F, E, S, It.

2007-08: Na, Ge, F (2), Ar, It, S, W, E, NZ.

2008-09: C, NZ, Ar, F, It, E, S, W.

Wallace Paddy (16)

2006-07: SA, PI, E, Ar.

2007-08: S (2), Na, E, NZ, A.

2008-09: C, NZ, F, It, E, W.

Key:

A (Australia); Ar (Argentina); C (Canada); E (England); F (France); Fi (Fiji); Ge (Georgia); It (Italy); J (Japan); NZ (New Zealand); PI (Pacific Islands); R (Romania); Ru (Russia); S

(Scotland); SA (South Africa); Sam (Samoa); T (Tonga); Us (USA); W (Wales); N (Namibia).

Appendix (ii)

Most Capped Players

All-Time Records – To March 2009

John Hayes	94
Brian O'Driscoll	93
Ronan O'Gara	92
Malcolm O'Kelly	92
Peter Stringer	89
Girvan Dempsey	82
David Humphreys	72
Kevin Maggs	70
Mike Gibson	69
Marcus Horan	66
Simon Easterby	65
Shane Horgan	64

Willie-John McBride	63
Geordan Murphy	63
Anthony Foley	62
Denis Hickie	62
Paul O'Connell	62
Fergus Slattery	61
Paddy Johns	59
Phil Orr	58
Keith Wood	58
Brendan Mullin	55
Donncha O'Callaghan	55
David Wallace	55
Peter Clohessy	54
Tom Kiernan	54
Donal Lenihan	52

Appendix (iii)

Top Try Scorers
To March 2009

Brian O'Driscoll	36
Denis Hickie	29
Shane Horgan	20
Girvan Dempsey	19
Geordan Murphy	18
Brendan Mullin	17
Kevin Maggs	15
Keith Wood	15
Ronan O'Gara	14
George Stephenson	14
Keith Crossan	12
Alan Duggan	11

Simon Geoghegan	11
David Wallace	11
Tommy Bowe	10
Hugo MacNeill	10
Mike Gibson	9
Joseph Quinn	9
Trevor Ringland	9
Jonathan Bell	8
Justin Bishop	8
Eugene Davy	8
Simon Easterby	8
John Kelly	8
Jim McCarthy	8

Appendix (iv)

Top Points Scorers
To March 2009

Ronan O'Gara	919
David Humphreys	560
Michael Kiernan	308
Eric Elwood	296
Ollie Campbell	217
Brian O'Driscoll	195
Tom Kiernan	158
Denis Hickie	145
Tony Ward	113
Mike Gibson	112
Paul Burke	108
Shane Horgan	100

Geordan Murphy	98
Girvan Dempsey	95
Ralph Keyes	94
George Stephenson	89
Richard Lloyd	75
Kevin Maggs	75
Keith Wood	75
Barry McGann	72
Brendan Mullin	72
David Wallace	55
Noel Henderson	54
Simon Geoghegan	51
Tommy Bowe	50

Appendix (v)

Top Kickers
To March 2009

Ronan O'Gara	317
David Humphreys	198
Eric Elwood	111
Michael Kiernan	102
Ollie Campbell	69
Tom Kiernan	57
Paul Burke	39
Tony Ward	36
Ralph Keyes	31
Mike Gibson	23
George Stephenson	20
Richard Lloyd	19

Barry McGann	18
Paddy Wallace	17
George Norton	16
Simon Mason	15
Noel Henderson	14
Paul Murray	11
James Parke	11
Anthony Ensor	9
Billy McCombe	9
Cecil Pedlow	9
Peter Russell	9
William Crawford	8
Barney Mullan	8

Appendix (vi)

Ireland's Five/Six Nations Record

Triple Crown

2009

2007

2006

2004

1985

1982

1949

1948

1899

1894

Champions

2009

1985

1983 (shared with France)

1982

1974

1973 (five-way tie)

1951

1949

1948

1939 (shared with Wales and England)

1935

1932 (shared with Wales and England)

1927 (shared with Scotland)

1926 (shared with Scotland)

1912 (shared with England)

1906 (shared with Wales)

1896

1894

Grand Slam

2009

1948

Bibliography

Irish Rugby Supporters Club, Dublin.

Irish Rugby Football Union, Dublin.

Radio Telefis Eireann

The Irish Times

The Irish Independent

The Evening Herald Dublin

BBC Sport

Daily Mail

Carling Opta Stats

The Guardian, Robert Kitson (Paul O'Connell)

The Sunday Independent, Brendan Fanning (Geordan Murphy and Denis Leamy)

The Sunday Times, Peter O'Rielly (Brian O'Driscoll)

Roy Curtis (Brian O'Driscoll);

Irish Times, John O'Sullivan (Jamie Heaslip)

Roy Curtis (Brian O'Driscoll);

Irish Independent (Declan Kidney's appointment)

Evening Herald, Dublin (Ireland Coaching staff)

Bebo.com (David Wallace)

Inpho/IRFU – squad details, (John Hayes) coaching staff profiles

Planet-rugby.com

www.Irishrugby.ie

www.Scrum.com